ROARING SILENCE

Roaring Silence

DISCOVERING THE MIND
OF DZOGCHEN

Ngakpa Chögyam
& Khandro Déchen

SHAMBHALA
Boston & London
2002

SHAMBHALA PUBLICATIONS, INC.
Horticultural Hall
300 Massachusetts Avenue
Boston, Massachusetts 02115
www.shambhala.com

©2002 by Ngakpa Chögyam and Khandro Déchen

9 8 7 6 5 4 3 2 1

First Edition
Printed in the United States of America

∞ This edition is printed on acid-free paper that meets the
American National Standards Institute Z39.48 Standard.

Distributed in the United States by Random House, Inc.,
and in Canada by Random House of Canada Ltd

Library of Congress Cataloging-in-Publication Data
Nga-kpa Chögyam.
    Roaring silence: discovering the mind of Dzogchen /
Ngakpa Chögyam and Khandro Déchen.—1st ed.
        p.   cm.
    ISBN 1-57062-944-7
    1. Rdzogs-chen (Räniçn-ma-pa)   I. Khandro Déchen.   II. Title.
BQ7662.4 .n49   2002
294.3'420423—dc21   2002005562

This book is dedicated to
Kyungchen Aro Lingma,
and to the gö-kar-chang-lo'i-dé,
the ngak'phang tradition of the Nga-gyür Nyingma.

If there is any value to be found in this book,
it is entirely due to the inspiration of the Nyingma lineages.
Any faults are entirely due to our own inadequacies.

Om A'a ᨀ Hung Bendzra Guru Jnana Sagara Bam Ha Ri Ni Sa
    Siddhi Hung ᨀ

Om A'a ᨀ Hung Bendzra Guru Pema Siddhi Hung ᨀ

Contents

CONTENTS

Foreword

SPIRITUAL TEACHINGS are living language, potent and transformative. Spiritual language confronts the hegemony of nihilism in its own stronghold, the domain of the thinking mind. Dharma teachings, Dharma books, are not to be read merely as an intellectual pastime but approached as windows into possibility, opening the mind's territory out beyond the confines of "egological" rationale.

In the Tibetan Vajrayana tradition, before studying a text, one receives a "reading" transmission from a master of the text. This reading transmission is received by hearing the text from the lips of one who has embodied its meaning—in whom the word has become lived experience. Transmission is the moment when communication becomes communion and information opens into the possibility of transformation. Transmission ensures that we understand that even the words themselves are alive with the potent force of the sacred. If we enter into the living vision expressed in books such as *Roaring Silence*, we discover ourselves to have become something other than what we were, but not yet what we can be. We enter into a view of potential realization but have not yet realized this view in the fullness of our lives. We become a pregnant space, and then, if we so choose, through meditation and action we can give birth to profound realization of our Buddha nature.

The great masters of Vajrayana have always understood that information alone does not bring about transformation. No amount of collected data will ever answer the question that humanity finds itself to be. What is conveyed through a Dharma teaching is not mere information but something subtler, less tangible. The language of Dharma flows from spirituality's lived experience as the natural impulse, energy, and thrust of compassion, and carries with it the subtle potency that is transmission. Such language not only affects our cognitive framework but acts upon the whole of our lives, our world, and our relationship to our world, through internalization of view. In the tradition of the Nyingma lineage, this power of language to communicate view is part of the triad of view, meditation, and action that constitutes the path. As Ngak'chang Rinpoche and Khandro Déchen express so well in the opening of this book: "In order to feel replete, the 'intellectual sense' needs to masticate, digest, and excrete. The intellectual appetite needs to be directed away from the processed abstractions of philosophical junk food. Intellect itself needs to taste the manner in which it functions as a method of obscuring the nature of Mind. . . . This is where the use of intellect stops being a pastime or a conspiratorial battlefield of conflicting notions. This is where intellect becomes a valuable tool with which we can begin to prompt interesting departures from the experiential myopia of the materialistic rationale. This is known as the development of view."

Dharma language, Dharma books are compassionate acts that arise from deeply lived experience of the teachings; they transport us, if we allow them to, into a new vision of life. They are the energy of compassion divulged through language. Spiritual teaching as transmission is the communication of a radical argument about the nature of existence and experience. In the Nyingma lineage of Vajrayana Buddhism, the view is not simply a set of good ideas but a dimension of being that is given expression through the power of compassion. As Ngak'chang Rinpoche and Khandro Déchen so aptly put it, "View is the collected experience of almost three thousand years of meditation practice in which a great number of *yogi*s and *yogini*s have made the same discovery. View comprises the mechanical functioning of unenlightenment and the nature of the enlightened state insofar as it can be expressed in language. So, view consists of seeing how we are in terms of our disquiet, dissatisfaction, confusion, frustration, irritation, and pain. But view also consists of glimpsing the nature of the enlightened state insofar as it can be pointed at by oral, symbolic, and direct transmission." View, a vision of existence based in direct perception and participation with truth, becomes the womb-space of realization. One's own Buddha nature, full-blown and complete, is born from this womb like the winged *garuda* that emerges as a fully mature and complete being able to soar into the vast openness of space. The potential for realization is fertilized through transmission, nurtured in the womb-space of view, and matured through meditation, and it flies in the dimension of action.

In the information age, language is often reduced to the mechanical conveyance of bits of data. Such language, suffering under the deadly force of reductionism, is stripped of its life-bearing, meaning-enhancing mystery and power. It contains no force of transmission. Words become mere facts and data streams, information good only for commerce. The teachings of Buddhadharma, in contrast, are living language, both medium and message, opening a view beyond the narrow confines of nihilistic materialism.

This idea of language as a means of transformation, rather than simply a communication of facts, is not unique to Eastern thought. The Greek god Hermes personified the transformative power of living language. Hermes, the god of thresholds and crossings, of twilight lands of the liminal state, did not convey mundane messages of insignificant import but delivered "fateful tidings." These fateful tidings were sufficiently potent to push mortals over a threshold that forever transformed the course of their lives. The Buddha's message is just such a fateful tiding. To approach a Dharma book correctly is to listen to and hear the radical argument of the Buddha and to be changed, to be pushed over a threshold, and to discover oneself in a different vision of life. In the information age, with its glut of meaningless data, we can lose sight of the truth that language can be of radical import and that books can provide doorways into new realms. The book you hold in your hands is an invitation, a doorway, a threshold.

Until one hears the message of Hermes, one's life remains pretty much the same. There may be adventures and seemingly profound insights, but they always take place within the context of what is already known. It is when Hermes delivers his fateful tidings that possibilities arise from outside of what could ever have been imagined. The Buddha's message to humanity is a radical intervention in the ordinary affairs of life's fictions. This message is not technocratic language conveying facts and figures but a vision in words; it is language as experience. It was Martin Heidegger who rediscovered (for this has been known and lost throughout the ages and cultures of humankind) that language is not simply a mechanism for the description of experience but a form of experience itself. In *On the Way to Language,* Heidegger explains that human beings, in the depths of their humanity, are striving to listen for the message delivered by Hermes. The question that humanity finds itself to be urges us into a deep listening and quest for a vision, a view that moves beyond the narrow confines of nihilist dogmas and into wondrous dimensions of being—and even into that mystery beyond being. Humankind waits for fateful tidings that offer up the possibility of an answer to the question posed by existence. View, in the triad of view, meditation, and action, is that answer framed in language. The view of the Nyingma lineage's inner Tantras is so piercing and radical, so astounding and profound, that to enter its argument takes all we have. This listening, this imbibing of view, requires much from a reader who is not content with the shallow spiritual materialism found in the extraction of mechanistic techniques.

Most readers will not find themselves in the dimension of magic that the ritual circumstance of an authentic reading transmission conjures. Short of this, it is the choice of each reader to engage the power and possibility of the text on his or her own. One might know the words simply through reading them, but one must enter into an intense dialogue in order to understand the fullness of the view. This dialogue must allow for profound questioning, in the light of the Buddha's radical argument, about the nature of being. One must allow the dialogue, as Heidegger puts it in *On the Way to Language,* to cause a questioning of "the guiding notions which, under the names 'expression,' 'experience,' and 'consciousness', determine modern thinking." This deep questioning, taking place at the heart of experience, is exactly the activity of shi-nè as described in this book. In the space of this questioning, the view of the inner Tantras of the Nyingma lineage becomes a womb-space for the realization of our Buddha nature. Without this womb-space of view, the place of spiritual practice would simply be conventional mind. Conventional mind has, as Chögyam Trungpa Rinpoche went to such pains to point out, great capacity to co-opt spiritual practice for its own purposes. Outside of the womb-space of view and transmission, the dynamic and organic process of skillful means suffers a deadly reductionism into mechanical technique at the hands of constricting intellectualisms. View, the vision of wholeness in which the resultant path of Tantra or the most radical path of Dzogpa Chenpo takes place, must always be established first as the ground of experience.

This womb-space is liminal, a space of transition. The anthropologist Victor Turner coined the term *liminality* as a "betwixt and between" state. Liminal comes from the Latin *limen,* meaning "threshold." The liminal state lies between two more relatively fixed dimensions of being. It is a bardo of sorts, a transitional process between death and rebirth. The view is not yet realization but a threshold between the tyranny of ordinary perceptions—a lived view shaped and molded by delusion—and the sublime open vistas of Buddhadharma. In other words, the view of Buddhadharma does not allow one to remain complacent in one's old vision, and yet, until one passes through the stages of meditation and integration, one is not able to truly realize this new view in terms of lived experience. One is betwixt and between—one is dying to an old vision and being reborn in a new one.

One cannot give birth to realization without having internalized the view, but the view is not sufficient without meditation and action. The Buddha's radical argument with and against delusion is the beginning of a long journey through the stages of meditation and action. The radical argument of the Buddha shatters our rigid vision of self-existent dualities. The sublime teachings of the Nyingma lineage's inner Tantras open our view into vistas of wonderment. But this new vision will not give birth to realization without living transmission, meditation, and integration. Dharma books are not so much self-help books as invitations to enter into living lineages of transmission. The transformation that you are invited to in this book requires far more than reading.

In 1584, the samurai Lord Nabeshima wrote on a wall a series of inscriptions outlining the path. The first and foremost of these said, "Intelligence is the flower of discrimination. There are many examples of the flower blooming but not bearing fruit." In the Zen tradition, one often hears stories of the empty or full teacup. The full cup, which symbolizes the mind filled with its own prejudices, cannot receive the teachings, but the empty teacup has the necessary spaciousness to receive teachings with ease. In the lineage of Do Khyentsé Yeshé Dorje, there is a wonderful story of Do Khyentsé forcing upon a scholar-monk a meal so large that the man begins to vomit. Do Khyentsé then explains to the man that his undigested knowledge, which he vomits onto others, is just like this meal. With compassion Do Khyentsé then offers to teach him the secret of proper digestion. The first step, which is equivalent to hearing the argument contained in the words of this book, is to allow wisdom to intervene in the cold comfort of delusion's tyranny.

The Buddha's teaching is the most radical intervention in ordinary affairs in human history. The inner Tantras and the view of Dzogchen are the quintessence of this intervention. The uncompromising nature of the Buddha's esoteric instructions are, if their import is truly heard, a shock and even an affront to the egological foundation of existence. To encounter view and allow its argument to sparkle through our delusion is to have the entire body of our life and world changed as radically as the body of a woman is changed by pregnancy. It demands that we question our assumptions to their very core.

Such questioning is demanding and often unsettling. Not all attempts at pregnancy succeed. Most people read the words of a Dharma book or listen to a Dharma talk but never fully grasp the meaning so that it becomes their own lived experience. Sometimes people attempt to reduce the Vajrayana path to mechanical techniques that can be bought and sold in the marketplace of spiritual consumerism, then find that their meditation bears no fruit. View, as conveyed in authentic teachings such as this book, is neither simple nor always gentle. Sometimes it insults our most cherished notions and drags the dark corners of our life into the glaring sun of self-examination. There is no internalization of view without disillusionment. Chögyam Trungpa Rinpoche often said that the starting point is hopelessness. To be disillusioned, to be disabused of our illusions, is part and parcel of hearing the Buddha's radical argument. There is nothing abstract about the Buddha's argument, for it is an argument with who we are, as sentient beings, and how we have adapted to a life based on the axioms of delusion. There is no birth without a powerful disruption of the status quo.

The conception, gestation, and birth of something so subtle as the realization of our Buddhahood is facilitated by the most delicate of circumstances. To coax human beings from the narrow labyrinths of constricted conceptuality and its endless self-justifying loops of pseudologic is no simple endeavor. "Question Everything" makes a nice bumper sticker but is quite difficult to embody if one is to take it beyond the confines of adolescent rebellion. To imbibe the view of the Nyingma tradition of Tantra and Dzogchen requires extraordinarily sensitive insight, understanding, courage, independence of thought, and a willingness to have the rug pulled out from under our most cherished assumptions. The egological rationale that defends the territory of delusion's stronghold has many built-in protection systems that work to ensure that view and meditation do not take root deeply. In the practice of shi-nè, which this book outlines, these protection systems can be summed up by the words *boredom*, *discomfort*, and *doubt*.

When conditioned responses, shaped by the endless spin of the mind's fictions, encounter the radical nature of the Buddha's doctrine, the mind shimmies and shakes while trying to get off the hook of uncompromising compassion. The addictions and consolations of samsara are sweet in the beginning and bitter in the end. Conversely, the radical argument of the Buddha oftentimes seems bitter when first encountered, but when we fully embrace its wisdom, we come to know the sweet fragrance of the flower of truth and compassion. In the face of meditation's obstacles, it is the view, as internalized in deep dialogue with authentic teachings, that buttresses our resolve not to be tricked yet again by samsara's seductions. For view to fulfill this role, it must not be shallow intellectual information. Boredom, discomfort, and doubt will shatter such a foundation in a matter of moments. View must be whole-body knowing arising from the force of profound listening and deep dialogue.

Information is not transformation. This book is not meant to provide you with some second-hand information with which to bolster the spiritual knowledge you may feel you have acquired. It is an invitation to mystery. *Roaring Silence* is born from compassion's urge to communicate. It is born from the word made flesh and the flesh of lived experience communicated to yet another generation and culture through the living power of language. This is the mystery and secret of lineage. Ngak'chang Rinpoche and Khandro Déchen invite us to join a primordial dialogue. They cajole, provoke, and seduce us with their expressions of wisdom by whispering unsettling propositions into our ears. Ngak'chang Rinpoche and Khandro Déchen do not attempt to adjust the view or method to suit the demands of the spiritual materialist or consumerist culture. Without bowing to the demands of delusion's marketing analysis, these two Lamas count on the natural innate mind of wisdom to sparkle through our delusion just enough to entice us into accepting their offer.

If view is the womb-space, and meditation and action nurture the birth of spontaneous self-liberating, self-recognizing wisdom, then Ngak'chang Rinpoche and Khandro Déchen are the best of midwives. Trained, accomplished, and compassionate, they offer us an introductory exploration of the view and its methods. The clarity of their words speaks of their own deep practice and understanding of this process. Their humor and lightheartedness betoken the ease and openness so often found in those who have shaped their lives to the view. Their seriousness and unwillingness to compromise with the heart of the method display their courage and sincerity.

Roaring Silence does not offer a do-it-yourselfer's guide to enlightenment but rather an invitation to enter the debate between the miasma of conditioned fictions that rule our lives and the pure, vast, open sublimity of the Buddha's gift. Like Hermes crossing borders in twilight to deliver the fateful tidings, Ngak'chang Rinpoche and Khandro Déchen conjure words into living vision, slipping the Buddha's message past the border guards of ego's dictatorship and directly into the heart of our lives. Read carefully. You just might become pregnant.

Traktung Yeshé Dorje
Guru Rinpoche Day, March 2002

Acknowledgments

WE GRATEFULLY ACKNOWLEDGE all our Lamas, but especially: H.H. Dudjom Rinpoche, H.H. Dilgo Khyentsé Rinpoche, Kyabjé Künzang Dorje Rinpoche and Jomo Sam'phel, and Kyabjé Chhi'mèd Rig'dzin Rinpoche.

Heartfelt love and respect to our vajra sisters Jétsunma Khandro Ten'dzin Drölkar and Khandro Tséring Wangmo.

And to our vajra brothers: Tharchin Rinpoche, Gyaltsen Rinpoche, Ngak'chang La-kar Chö-kyi Wangchuk Rinpoche, Tulku Thubten Rinpoche, and Phüntsog Tulku.

We thank our vajra sangha of ordained ngak'phang disciples: Ngakma Nor'dzin Rang-jung Pamo, Nga-la Rig'dzin Taklung Rolpa'i Dorje, Ngakpa 'ö-Dzin Tridral 'ö-Zér Nyima Dorje, Ngakma Shardröl Du-nyam Ja'gyür Rang-tsal Chhi'mèd Wangmo, Ngakma Yeshé Zér-tsal Wangmo, Naljorma Jig'mèd Khyungtsal Pamo, Naljorpa Rang-rig Long-tsal Dorje, and Naljorma 'ö-Sel Nyima Chèrdröl Khandro.

We would like to thank our vajra family of apprentices, and the apprentices of Nga-la Rig'dzin Taklung Rolpa'i Dorje; and Ngakma Nor'dzin Rang-jung Pamo and Ngakpa 'ö-Dzin Tridral 'ö-Zér Nyima Dorje.

Finally, many thanks to all the friends of the registered charities within the Confederate Sanghas of Aro: Sang-ngak-chö-dzong in Britain, Aro Gar in the U.S.A., Aro Gesellschaft in Austria, and Aro Gemeinschaft in Germany.

ROARING SILENCE

Introduction

ZOGCHEN IS THE vastness of each moment.[1] It is the natural simplicity of being which, in itself, is the only teaching or practice. Dzogchen, the pinnacle of all Nyingma[2] teachings, makes this declaration of natural simplicity as the lion's roar of reality.[3] The lion's roar leaves no doubt. Such a roar is not a threat, although it inevitably intimidates those who have taken refuge in timidity. The lion, however, does not give voice to reality in order to intimidate— its roar is simply a roaring silence: the self-existent proclamation of self-existent confidence. This confidence, which is naturally ours, is the empty confidence that has no need of reference points.[4] It is the confidence that makes itself known within the subatomic structure of our experience.

Dzogchen proclaims the self-existent confidence[5] of all beings— as they essentially are. The enlightened state is simply there as the basis of what we are. The roaring silence of this utter totality is the empty thread upon which the glittering beads of each moment of our being string themselves. *Utter totality* is a term that applies to both teaching

1. Dzogchen (rDzogs chen) means "utter totality." It is also translated as "great completion," "great completeness," or "great perfection."
2. Nyingma (rNying ma) is the Old Translation tradition of Vajrayana Buddhism. It was established by Padmasambhava and Yeshé Tsogyel in the ninth century.
3. seng-gé'i dra (seng ge'i sGra).
4. Reference points are "proofs of existence," za té (gZa' gTad).
5. gyukyen gyi sar du ma ye pa (rGyu rKyen gyi gSar du ma byas pa).

and practice and to the intrinsic condition of the individual. The teaching of Dzogchen declares that meditation *is* the state of relaxation—a means by which we can be *what we are*, without tension, tyranny, or anxiety. According to this view, there is nothing to change—nothing to give up or alter in any way. We simply need to be what we are. Simply being what we are, without manipulation or struggle, is all that is necessary.

These are bold yet simple statements—but if we are not particularly simple people, what will we make of them? Further investigation may be required. We do not intend to purvey a continuing series of rapturous statements that may merely intoxicate or weary the reader. It is not our aim to confuse—but maybe we need to explore confusion in order to get some glimpse of the vast sky of awareness in which confusion hides.

Dzogchen means *utter totality*. Dzogchen also describes a body of teaching. It is a system of catalysts. It describes the fundamental nature of *what we are* through simply opening the roof of our perception. Dzogchen encourages us to approach our essential nature directly—because that essential nature is so close, so accessible, so present, and so simple. It is possible—but that in itself is the major barrier. It is also *too* close, *too* accessible, *too* present, and *too* simple—for people as complex as we find ourselves to be. The complexity of the "unenlightenment" we appear to experience would seem to contradict these marvelous assertions of our closeness to the realized state.

So it would seem that we cannot approach Dzogchen directly. Or if we can, it is with a type of directness that is so different from what we understand by "direct" that there is nothing direct about it. We have a paradox,[6] and wherever there is a paradox, metaphors and symbols are apparently helpful. It would seem that we might need explanations that are as elaborate as we would appear to be. It should be possible simply to give this teaching in five words: *remain in the natural state*. From the perspective of Dzogchen, that should be enough. It should be enough merely to hear that. Then, on hearing it, we

6. dog-drö (lDog 'gros), paradox.

should be able to allow everything to relax into its own condition. But what can such statements mean to us in terms of our everyday experience of silent sitting? From the dualistic perspective, they leave many questions unanswered.[7] They also seem to create a broad variety of new questions.

Often we are so immured within the relentless censorship of intellect that simplicity can become a complex matter. The complexity of intellect can impose such severe restraints on our perceptions that the instruction "remain in the natural state" is rendered incomprehensible. Thinking about such a proposition does not help, so we have to abandon our attempts to understand on the basis of what we already comprehend, and that leaves us with the roaring silence of meditation.

Meditation enables us to sidestep the bureaucracy of rigid intellectual processes and experience ourselves directly. But before being sidestepped, the intellect needs to be fed a little. The intellect needs real food if it is to satiate itself adequately. In order to feel replete, the "intellectual sense" needs to masticate, digest, and excrete.[8] The intellectual appetite needs to be directed away from the processed abstractions of philosophical junk food. Intellect itself needs to taste the manner in which it functions as a method of obscuring the nature of Mind. (*Mind*, when given a capital *M*, relates to the emptiness quality of being rather than the content of Mind. The lowercase-*m* mind relates to the mind with which we are familiar in terms of dualistic perceptions, judgments, and feelings.) This is where the use of intellect stops being a pastime or a conspiratorial battlefield of conflicting ideas. This is where intellect becomes a valuable tool with which we can begin to prompt interesting departures from the experiential myopia of the materialistic rationale. This is where we can give birth

7. Duality refers to the state in which enlightenment and unenlightenment, security and insecurity, existence and nonexistence (the word pairs are limitless) are experienced as divided.

8. Dzogchen regards ideation or intellectual sensing as one of the senses, just as seeing, hearing, fragrance sensing, tasting, and touch sensing. We "see," "hear," "sniff," "savor," and "feel" with thought in terms of apprehending the world.

to the possibility of looking directly into the nature of Mind. Through study, through wholesome inquisitive skepticism, we can arrive at the point where looking directly into the nature of Mind becomes a feasible proposition. This is known as the development of view.

View is the collected experience of almost three thousand years of meditation practice in which a great number of *yogis* and *yoginis*[9] have made the same discovery. View comprises the mechanical functioning of unenlightenment and the nature of the enlightened state insofar as it can be expressed in language. So, view consists of seeing how we are in terms of our disquiet, dissatisfaction, confusion, frustration, irritation, and pain. But view also consists of glimpsing the nature of the enlightened state insofar as it can be pointed at by oral, symbolic, and direct transmission.[10]

In the Dzogchen view, which concerns the nature of Mind, the approach is highly pragmatic. The view holds the same pragmatism as does the art of lighting a fire—no one ever got colder sitting in front of a fire. And no one ever succeeded in making a fire using pebbles and river water. When we know how to allow a fire to spring into being by mixing wood and oxygen through the medium of heat, we do not need to remember the exact wording of the instruction booklet—we simply create fire. As soon as we integrate the view, the view disappears and becomes knowledge. Knowledge is like breathing—we do not have to remember how to breathe. So, view is a way of employing intellect to transcend intellect. To this end, view must always be tested in the laboratory of our own experience. This is the creative use of intellect in which we confront the day-to-day sensation of what we are. Because the intellect is a genuine faculty, it can become untangled. This book is an exploration of how we are as

9. Naljorpas and naljormas (rNal 'byor pa and rNal 'byor ma) are those who practice the inner yogas.
10. The three styles of transmission (communication of the enlightened state) as defined within the Dzogchen teachings are oral transmission, or nyen gyüd (sNyan brGyud); symbolic transmission, or da gyüd (brDa brGyud)—either formal symbolic (shedlung da, bShad lung brDa) or informal symbolic (gyu-kyen da, rGyu rKyen brDa); and direct (or Mind-to-Mind) transmission, or gong gyüd (dGongs brGyud).

beings tangled in complexities, and of how we are as beings becoming untangled.

To begin this exploration we are going to look at the three crucial aspects of the path. In the Dzogchen tradition these are known as view, meditation, and action.[11] *View* provokes or incites our natural intelligence. *Meditation* opens our realization to the view. *Action* is the pure appropriateness of our spontaneity in the state of realization. Meditation enables us to find out for ourselves.

It is deliciously and painfully amusing that at the ultimate level we are our own greatest teachers. It is deliciously amusing because sometimes everything seems to unfold spontaneously—we seem to flow easily with circumstances. It is painfully amusing because the irony of our situation makes its own point and sometimes we cannot help noticing this. In some ways, we are setting out to stand conventional logic on its head, but this does not mean that there is no place in this process for intelligent reasoning. We merely need to allow an unlearning process to inaugurate itself—a process in which habits of compulsive attachment to conditioned patterns of intellect start to become transparent.[12] The reach and range of reasoning mind is quite small and, although it is capable of remarkable feats, it cannot give us access to all the answers. Let us take an example. It could well be considered that thinking is not a particularly effective way of dealing with emotional pain. Thinking about emotional pain invariably generates thoughts that run circles around themselves, generating more thoughts. Thinking about emotionally painful experiences seems only to make matters worse. It never appears to bring us nearer to an understanding of what we are individually experiencing. Thinking about pain merely constitutes "thinking around it"—that is to say, thinking about the circumstances that surround the pain.

Apart from certain psychotherapeutic contexts, people seldom think about pain itself. The reason for this is that if we were to think

---

11. tawa (lTa ba), gompa (sGom pa), and chopa (spyod pa).
12. zang-tal lé (zang thal le), transparent—the transparence of that which arises in Mind (see chapters 9 and 10).

about pain itself, we would unavoidably enter the language of pain. Thought is not capable of bringing us to an understanding of the fundamental texture of pain. We can only investigate pain with the nonconceptual observation of meditation. Thoughts merely create a barrier—as if "pain" and "the experiencer of pain" were separate. Most people will be familiar with the way in which circular thoughts keep them awake at night, even when their greatest wish is to sleep. Human beings are evidently addicted to the process of thought, and as with any kind of addiction, there is a necessity to consider the consequences of the habit. What we are about to embark upon is an exploration of this habit.

Roaring Silence is a handbook of the *Aro Naljor-zhi*—the Four Naljors. We use the term *handbook* because exercises are given in a manner that can be followed and because advice is given on the typical experiences that arise when following them. However, the reader should not assume that the Four Naljors can be encapsulated within a handbook. Transmission is required and should eventually be sought.

The Four Naljors are the *ngöndro,*[13] or preliminary practices, for Dzogchen Sem-dé.[14] Sem-dé is one of the three "series" of Dzogchen. It contains the most extensive body of teaching on *sem*, conceptual mind, and *sem-nyid*, the nature of Mind. The Four Naljors are methods that enable the development of the necessary experiences through

13. Ngöndro (sNgon 'gro)—literally, "before going," usually translated as preparation, foundation, or preliminary—is required for every level of practice if one has not arrived at the level of experience that allows one to enter directly into the experiences indicated by the teaching. The word *ngöndro* is used to describe many different kinds of practice, and Sem-dé-pa'i ngöndro zhi should not be confused with Gyüd-pa'i ngöndro zhi, the four Tantric preparatory practices.

14. Series of the nature of Mind. Sem (sems) is a contraction of the word *sem-nyid* (sems nyid), the nature of Mind. *Dé* (sDe) means "series." *Sem-dé* has sometimes been incorrectly translated as "mental series" or "mental class" by those unfamiliar with Dzogchen terminology. This is due to the fact that the word *sem* literally means "conceptual mind." Within the Dzogchen teaching, however, *sem* is used as a contraction of the term *sem-nyid*. Sem in Dzogchen terminology also relates to changchub-sem (byang chub sems), or *bodhicitta*—the "heart-mind of the state of enlightenment."

which Dzogchen becomes practicable. The word *naljor* literally means "natural state remaining."[15] So in ordinary contemporary English, the Four Naljors are the four methods of remaining in the natural state.

The Four Naljors are composed of the practices of shi-nè,[16] lha-tong, nyi'med, and lhun-drüp.[17] We will introduce shi-nè without further ado, but lha-tong, nyi'med, and lhun-drüp will need to await definition in the following chapters, where their practice will be given in detail. Shi-nè is the method for freeing oneself from addictive referential attachment to the thought process. This is the basic method of meditation according to the Four Naljors. It is also found in the other traditions of Tibetan practice.[18] Wherever shi-nè is taught it concerns the relaxation of involvement with internal dialogue. It concerns letting go of the mental gossip that inhibits direct perception. Shi-nè is the treatment for our addiction to thought patterns. If you decide to enter into this treatment, the first thing you may find is that it can be boring. It is crucial to understand this: shi-nè can be boring. Shi-nè can be irritating. It can be frustrating. It can be deadly tedious, especially in the initial stages, and especially if you are an active, intelligent, creative human being. This is because practicing shi-nè is "going without a fix." The experience has some slight similarity to the cold turkey experienced by heroin addicts who abjure from injecting. This comparison may sound a little extreme, but to anyone who has ever entered into the practice with commitment, it will seem fairly apt as a description of some of the very worst moments—especially in retreat. Thought-attachment withdrawal

15. This is the etymological meaning of *naljor. Naljor* is a contraction of the words *rNal ma* (natural state) and *'byor pa* (remaining). This word is also used in Tantra to translate the Sanskrit word *yoga,* which means union, unifying, or unification. But in Dzogchen terminology the meaning relates to remaining in the natural state.

16. Shi-nè (zhi gNas) is pronounced *shee-neh.* The *e* in the final syllable is short and clipped as in the word *emptiness.*

17. lhag mThong, gNyis med, and lhun sGrub.

18. Shi-nè is found in all schools of Buddhism. In the formless Mahamudra of the Kagyüd school, it is called tséd-chig (rTse gCig), one-pointedness. In Zen Buddhism, it is the initial phase of *zazen.*

symptoms can be emotionally fraught and can make people want to give up almost as soon as they have begun to practice. But the appalling alternative is to resign oneself to living life as a thought-attachment junkie. From the perspective of natural being, the world of the thought addict is actually much more distressing than the thought-attachment withdrawal process of shi-nè. Unlike the dreadful discomfort and distress of heroin withdrawal symptoms, however, thought-attachment withdrawal symptoms are a fertile field of self-discovery. Whatever you feel when you practice shi-nè is a fundamental expression of how you are.

When you confront yourself in shi-nè you are brought face to face with your insecurity, fear, loneliness, vulnerability, and bewilderment. These underlying tensions distort your being whether you practice shi-nè or not. To avoid the practice of shi-nè is not an answer. In fact, from the Buddhist perspective, no one actually has much choice in the situation. It is not really so different from the arrival of an electric bill. The bill can either be paid or it can be pushed under the doormat with the pretense that it never arrived. Pushing bills under the doormat is not an answer—either you pay the bill or your service is disconnected. If you find yourself in the midst of a battle, then whether you face the enemy or not is almost not an issue—the chances that an arrow or a bullet will find you are high. However, if you face the enemy, you can at least gain the measure of the situation. Like all analogies, these only hint at the meaning, and one should not elaborate on them too much. If one asks too many intellectual questions about analogies, the best of them fall to pieces. So, to practice shi-nè is to work directly with how you are. To practice shi-nè is to begin to live your life rather than letting your life "live" you. To practice shi-nè is to get back into the driver's seat—to open your eyes and see the world. With our eyes open, we realize that we no longer have to play blindman's buff with our emotions.

Clarity spontaneously arises from the discovery of openness within the practice of shi-nè. Loosening our white-knuckled grasp on the thought process enables thought itself to be more intimately experienced. We experience the color, tone, and texture of thought. These qualities arise because we develop sufficient experience of openness in which to see thought in a spatial context. We become transparent to ourselves. Motivation becomes simpler. A natural compassion arises, a compassion that does not need to be forced or fabricated—the first real taste of freedom.

Shi-nè does not depend on accepting dogmas or elaborate Asiatic philosophies. The teachings of the Dzogchen Sem-dé ngöndro do describe a view, but it is a view that must be validated through experience. The view must be *real-ized*. As far as the simple practice of shi-nè is concerned, belief in Buddhism is not required, nor for that matter is there a need to believe in anything.

We belong to the Nyingma tradition of Tibetan Buddhism, and the methods outlined are part of that tradition. People who belong to other religious traditions may well benefit from the practices we outline, but we cannot offer advice as to how the Four Naljors might function in the context of paths we have not personally followed. The practice of shi-nè as we describe it exists within the context of the Nyingma yogic tradition. Nyingma yogis and yoginis practice shi-nè in conjunction with many other practices. These other practices involve the generation of compassion and the development of devotion toward one's Lama and lineage. (We would advise those who are seriously interested in the Four Naljors to seek instruction from a Lama—one who has a good command of the English language—at some stage in relation to the practices in this book, especially for the more advanced practices. Working alone for more than a few years would prove too difficult and discouraging. Ultimately, one requires transmission from a qualified, empowered Lama, or the actual practice of Dzogchen will bear no fruit.) People who try to practice spiritual methods out of context with the religious tradition that gave rise to them often find themselves lacking the impetus to maintain a regular practice. Without a regular practice it is difficult to get anywhere. Lacking the background of a religious context, people often find that their basic enthusiasm for the discipline of meditation dissipates.

Certainly, without the richness and support of a religious tradition, it proves difficult to persevere through the times when one's practice seems "unrewarding." From our experience, one has to belong somewhere. One has to be part of something that is sufficiently bigger than oneself in order to find support in a higher, deeper, broader context. One requires a context that goes beyond the isolated island of "me and my process."

Vajrayana Buddhism is obviously the religion of choice for these practices, because Vajrayana is the religion from which these practices originate. Furthermore, it is likely that those who consider themselves to be Nyingma practitioners will derive more inspiration from the living color of these practices than will even a person of another Tibetan tradition. These are not value judgments; they are merely pragmatic statements designed to be helpful rather than to confine, alienate, or exclude. Inspiration is crucial to maintaining a practice such as shi-nè, so one needs to address the issue of where and how one derives one's inspiration. Until you find yourself working with a Lama, of whatever tradition, you will be working on your own. Working on your own is not necessarily contraindicated in the very beginning, so it is possible to begin employing shi-nè in order to gain an understanding of what you are. If you approach practice in this way, then when you do have the opportunity of meeting a Lama, you will have real experiential questions to ask—and these questions will come from "you."

Buddhism isn't structured to promote belief in Buddhism. The Sutrayana in particular is an experiential science that encourages us to test everything. In the context of Sutrayana, Shakyamuni Buddha[19] stressed that people should not accept what he said just because he said it. Although the Four Naljors do not stem from Sutrayana,

19. The Buddha of the Sutric vehicle. The Buddhas of Tantra were Padmasambhava and Yeshé Tsogyel. The Buddha of Dzogchen was Garab Dorje. These Buddhas were the first human teachers of these vehicles. (In the case of the Aro gTér, Yeshé Tsogyel is the Dzogchen Buddha with regard to being the origin of the gTérma cycles taught by Aro Lingma.)

the approach of shi-nè equates with Sutra. Because shi-nè equates with Sutra, Shakyamuni Buddha's injunction that we should test his teaching rigorously against our own experience is vital. The Lama does not ask us to sell our integrity but rather to sell our limitations in order to discover ourselves on our journey into vastness.

QUESTIONS AND ANSWERS

(*Editor's note:* All questions and answers are taken from discussions between the authors and students at formal teaching events.)

QUESTION: You said that the reasoning mind was capable of remarkable feats but that it can't give you all the answers . . . Could you elaborate on that?

NGAKPA CHÖGYAM RINPOCHE: Intellect is form, and form is limited. Form is infinite in its variety, but you can't access everything with it. It's not a cerebral American Express card. There are unimaginable vistas beyond the reasoning mind to which intellect has no visa, and this is something that must be experienced *directly*—or missed completely. The nature of Mind is empty and therefore unlimited.

KHANDRO DÉCHEN: If we get stuck at the level of intellect, we cut ourselves off from the rich source of intellect's potentiality. The capacity for intellect itself arises from emptiness, and so in order to have free intellect, we need to move beyond intellect.

Q: When you say that we're able to experience the color, tone, and texture of thought, you seem to be describing it as if it were like one of the five senses.

KD: Thought is a sense. Concept consciousness *is* one of the sense fields. It's a mistake to conceive of cognition as if it were something quite different from the other sense fields. That idea is basic to Tantra.

It is also vital in terms of meditation, because it can be highly problematic to feel, or think, as if we operate always through the head.

NCR: We treat the brain as if it were the headquarters, or the central administration of everything, but that is not accurate, to say the least.

Q: I can understand how a feeling can have color and texture, but how is a thought like a feeling or sense?

KD: But what do you mean by feeling? It sounds as if you're dividing feeling from thought.

Q: Well, yes, I thought they were different.

KD: They can be, but that's not usually the case. Most people's feelings are impregnated by a thought. In fact, most people's emotions are thoroughly governed by thought. If feeling can have color and texture, then thought can have color and texture.

NCR: The sense fields can also be much like each other. In many shamanic traditions, the overlapping of the sense fields is encouraged, and many of the altered states that can be induced by one means or another open up the possibility of seeing sound, hearing color, and so on. This is really not so unusual. The main point, however, is that you don't really have to intellectually comprehend that thoughts can have color, tone, and texture. That's simply something you will discover when thoughts arise out of the condition of *mi-thogpa*, the state without thought.

Q: This thought-withdrawal process you describe sounds quite difficult—coming face to face with insecurity, fear, loneliness, bewilderment, etc. I would assume that this process varies greatly depending on the individual.

KD: Yes, certainly. But the discomfort always has the same kind of feelings associated with it. It's simply the intensity that varies.

PART ONE

AN INTRODUCTION

CHAPTER I

Sky and Mind

We need humor in order to avoid taking ourselves quite so seriously; we need to be able to laugh at the fact that we continually create our own unenlightened condition. Without humor we would not be able to relate to the idea that a Lama could comprehend the comedy of our personal dualism in an effective manner, and conjure with it to our advantage.

PREPARATION IS ESSENTIAL unless one has experience of emptiness.[1] Beyond that, it is essential to have some glimpse of the nondual nature of emptiness and form. Emptiness is the base of Tantra. The nondual state is the base of Dzogchen. Therefore, before Dzogchen can be approached as a path, one has to arrive at the base from which the path begins. This does not mean that one must be enlightened to be able to approach this vehicle, but one must have *some* experience of its nondual base. This experience may simply consist of a series of brief flashes—but the experience must be there or one will merely flounder.

One must have arrived at the base of any vehicle one wishes to practice—and there is no knowing how many years of preparation it may take to arrive at that ground of experience. For Dzogchen to become viable for the individual, certain experiential criteria must

1. Emptiness here equates to the experience of mi-thogpa, the absence of thought.

be satisfied. Otherwise, the methods that are called Dzogchen will merely be affectations.

Roaring Silence is a practical investigation of the criteria that must be met in terms of the experiential qualifications of the individual. These experiential qualifications are not imposed by Dzogchen as a Tibetan tradition—they are self-existent demands. If one does not meet these self-existent demands, one will be barred from the path *by the path itself.* Although preparation is required, there is no fixed, conceptually based law that dictates the exact nature of what will bring a person to the necessary base of experience. Different traditions make different requirements of the individual, and one should take direction from one's Lama. Having expressed these precautions, however, we should state once more that Dzogchen is the primordial state of the individual—and therefore everyone is primordially qualified as having the requisite base. We have all arrived at this point with our unique patterns of past-life experience, and there is no telling what latent capacities an individual may possess.

Let us now look at the question of preparation. Because Dzogchen Sem-dé can be approached through its own unique ngöndro, the Tantric ngöndro of the fourfold 100,000 practices of devotion, generosity, purification, and nonduality are not an indispensable prerequisite for Dzogchen—unless this has been categorically stated by one's own Lama.[2] Although Tantric ngöndro is not mandatory for the practice of Dzogchen Sem-dé, it should be clearly understood that the *result* of Tantric ngöndro is always necessary. If one wishes to practice Dzogchen, one has to arrive at its base—by whatever means is recommended by one's Lama.

Different lineages and different Lamas have their own particular approaches, and one cannot proceed without advice as to the path one chooses to follow. The Lama is integral and essential with regard

2. The Tantric ngöndro involves the 100,000 prostrations with refuge and bodhicitta, the 100,000 mandala offerings, the 100,000 recitations of the Dorje Sempa hundred-syllable mantra, and the 100,000 practices of Lama'i Naljor, or guru yoga.

to practice, and so all decisions about what is or is not necessary depend on one's own Lama.[3] It would be inappropriate, therefore, to take advice on this subject from a book—if that book conflicted with the advice one had received from one's chosen Lama. There is no purpose in requesting a Lama to accept one as a student and then to take issue with his or her advice on the basis of information received from other quarters. One chooses one's Lama on the basis of one's recognition of his or her qualities, and, having made the choice, one should remain steadfast in that choice.

The Four Naljors, which prepare the ground for the practice of Dzogchen Sem-dé in four ways, run parallel to the Tantric ngöndro in terms of their functional parameters. So, whether one practices according to one system or another, assiduous preparations are crucial. The Tantric ngöndro is the first stage of a symbolic method of arriving at the base of Dzogchen, and the Four Naljors ngöndro is a non-symbolic approach. Both approaches are characterized by the vehicle for which they are the foundation practice. The Tantric ngöndro has the character of Tantra, and its innermost practice is the heart of Tantra. Likewise, the Four Naljors ngöndro has the character of Dzogchen, and its innermost practice is the heart of Sem-dé, the nature of Mind series of Dzogchen.

Here we are faced with both possibility and impossibility in terms of approaching Dzogchen, but we could be so audacious as to approach it together if we had sufficient humor, inspiration, and determination. We require humor in order to be able to laugh at our own situation—to laugh at the conceptual limitations we experience. We need humor in order to avoid taking ourselves quite so seriously; we need to be able to laugh at the fact that we continually create our own unenlightened condition. Without humor, we would not be able to relate to the idea that a Lama could comprehend the

3. See Ngakpa Chögyam, *Wearing the Body of Visions* (New York & London: Aro Books, 1995), chapters 5 and 6, and Rig'dzin Dorje, *Dangerous Friend* (Boston: Shambhala Publications, 2001), which discuss the role of the Lama in detail.

comedy of our personal dualism in an effective manner, and conjure with it to our advantage. Hopefully, our discussions will provide some scope for such provocative humor.

We require inspiration in order to begin with our silent sitting and eventually seek out a Lama from whom to receive explicit guidance. Inspiration can only arise out of the sense in which something is possible. We have to catch a glimpse of "something" or we have to catch a glimpse of "no-thing." We must have our suspicion aroused with regard to the nature of what we are. To have looked for information, to have looked for a book, to have listened to a talk, to have attended teachings—all these are statements of inspiration. One would not be reading a book if inspiration were not there. All that remains is to feed that inspiration through the experiment of shi-nè.

We require determination in order to find ourselves at the base from which Dzogchen becomes possible. Determination is actually a mark of self-respect, a mark of innate dignity. Determination will naturally stem from the requisite humor and inspiration. Any person who intends to research the nature of his or her own being needs to have sufficient respect for the direction in which further discoveries lie. If one has actually glimpsed the possibility that there is something remarkable to be discovered, then no one with the requisite potential is going to slink back to the degraded confines of a bland experiential suburbia.

We require humor, inspiration, and determination in order to proceed. With these human qualifications, the impossibility of Dzogchen does not preclude the possibility of entering its living ethos. The ngöndro of Dzogchen Sem-dé is characterized by the ethos of Dzogchen, and we are able to live in both worlds—the world of the possible and the world of the impossible. This is called the starting point.

With regard to arriving at the starting point of Dzogchen,[4] it is essential to establish a relationship with a fully qualified Lama, but it is not impossible to begin to explore and to experiment with silent sitting. That is one purpose of this book, but we would also like to take

---

4. The starting point or base of Dzogchen is the experience of nonduality, and this is the goal that is attained through the Four Naljors.

you further in terms of what could be glimpsed. A book is limited, but reading a book can be an experience that prompts a journey. Our concern is merely to allow the transmissions we have received to inform the texture of the path as readers may experience it. There is a delicate balance involved in the presentation of a meditation manual, and we must be honest in saying that the possibility and impossibility of it will be an individual manifestation for each reader. Those with an existing devotional relationship with a Lama will certainly find themselves at an enormous advantage. So, although this book may be helpful, without authentic transmission one will not go very far beyond shi-nè. To have experienced the results of shi-nè, however, is an invaluable basis from which to request transmission. This in itself is extremely useful. So, having made the necessary caveats, let us begin.

We need to have a clear understanding of the principle and function of the Four Naljors, but we also have to understand very exactly what shi-nè is not. Before attempting to practice the Four Naljors, even at the level of shi-nè, it is necessary to engage in a little unlearning. Even for those with no particular misconceptions about shi-nè, it is possible to drift off course in terms of understanding. We are going to discuss the development of immunity to the diseases of distraction, distortion, and complication. There are many methods, in many religious and spiritual systems, that go by the name of "meditation," and this creates a certain difficulty in using that word. It is for this reason that we will not use the word very often. We will only use the word *meditation* as an umbrella term, in the context of discussing different techniques within the range of Tibetan meditative systems. In Tibetan, the word that equates to *meditation* is *gom* (sGom), and one has to be specific in terms of describing what kind of gom is being discussed. *rLung-gom* (rLung sGom), for example, is meditation that focuses on rLung, the spatial winds.[5] So specific methods will be introduced with specific Tibetan names. The first of these terms is shi-nè, which means "undisturbed" or "remaining uninvolved."[6]

5. Skt. prana.
6. Literally, "peaceful remaining," but often translated as "calm abiding."

Questions and Answers

QUESTION: Khandro Déchen, I was struck by what you said about Dzogchen becoming viable for the individual. I believe you said that particular experiential criteria must be satisfied or "the methods called Dzogchen" would be merely affectations. Could you say more about that?

KHANDRO DÉCHEN: Well, if you think about sexual maturity, for example, a base exists there, too. One has to have reached puberty. If young children were to see their parents making love and attempt to imitate their behavior, they would probably find it fairly uninteresting. There would be more interesting games for them to play. For Dzogchen to be viable, one has to have reached experiential maturity. If one has not reached the experiential maturity that encompasses nonduality—if only at the level of nascent tasting—then one cannot practice the outer form of the methods. By "outer methods" I am not simply referring to physical yogas or specific postures, I am talking about the instruction as to how to find the nature of Mind *as it is.* The outer method could be simply gazing into the sky and letting go of subject and object.

NGAKPA CHÖGYAM RINPOCHE: The description of the practice is simply the linguistic shell in which one would *find* the practice to be the nature of one's Mind. These are weighty considerations, but suffice it to say that a practice is not simply a practice. A practice as defined within Buddhism is always the union of the practice and the person practicing. There is no such thing as a practice that can be applied by anyone, irrespective of one's situation and motivation. A person with devotion to his or her Lama will experience these practices entirely differently from a person who has no relationship with a teacher.

Q: I'm wondering if that also applies to people who might teach. Could someone teach without having any actual experience?

KD: Yes, that is possible.

Q: How could you tell? This is important, isn't it?

KD: Very important, yes. You would tell by studying and practicing with such a person. You would have to test the teacher through your own practice.

NCR: And through observing the teacher in terms of being alert to incongruence. Incongruence might look like a person whose public persona was kindly and gentle and whose private behavior was petulant and aggressive. Incongruence might look like teachers who contradicted their own teachings within the fabric of their existence. It's a matter of using your basic street intelligence, really. We're not saying that teachers can't behave in extraordinary ways . . . we're just saying that you need to test the teacher according to the nature of the path itself, rather than some moralistic construct. Merely being able to express the teaching does not make someone a teacher. There has to be experience there, and the only way you can really find out whether there is real experience there is to study and practice. Most people do not really know enough about the teaching to test their teacher—but that is the best place to start. Not, we hasten to add, that it's useful to be suspicious.

KD: Yes, the process of testing should lead to greater devotion, because one comes to appreciate the true value of the Lama.

NCR: This testing is also "self-tested" testing, which means that it simply happens as a result of being real within the Lama-disciple relationship. If one practices with sincerity and with kind motivation, then the testing of which we speak will happen spontaneously.

Q: An idea that's become popular in recent years is that meditation is a type of therapy. What would you say about that in terms of shi-nè?

KD: For most people, unfortunately, the practice of shi-nè initially works with three things: drowsiness, unremitting "thought stories," and boredom. We are aware that we're making the practice of shi-nè sound uninviting. This is deliberate. We also wish to convey great enthusiasm for this practice, but that's a subtler task. It's a task that needs to be approached with greater honesty than one might expect in an attempt at a simplified presentation of the subject. It's all very well to make spiritual teachings more commonly available and to take advantage of the extraordinary possibilities inherent in publication, but some sense of ordinary effort needs to be understood. To proceed with this practice in a healthy and open-minded way, you may need to forget popular accounts you may have heard or read. If you practice shi-nè, you are not necessarily going to become a more relaxed human being within a week, a month, or even a year. This could be disappointing—but disappointment is a matter of perspective. The more you expect, the more disappointed you are likely to become.

Q: So you should attempt to expect very little.

KD: Yes, in fact, you should attempt to expect nothing at all—especially nothing special.

NCR: Anything you expect along the lines of "cosmic experience" is hardly likely to manifest—and if it does, it will probably have little connection with shi-nè.

KD: The first time one sits is bound to be something of a disappointment. But if your first sit is a big disappointment and you are prepared to continue, then you can begin to think of yourself as a potential practitioner. Anyone interested enough to be investigating this subject has the right qualifications to begin practicing shi-nè. Anyone interested enough to be reading this has the possibility of discovering what all enlightened beings have discovered.

NCR: To begin with, there is boredom. Then, after the boredom, there's yet more boredom [*laughs*].

KD: So, unless one is prepared to work with boredom, there is no purpose in considering the practice of shi-nè. If one is not prepared to sit through boredom as a continuing project, there is no way one can even begin practice. But, strangely enough, shi-nè is the only key to actually understanding boredom and discovering what life is like without it. Shi-nè is the means by which we comprehend boredom. Through practice, boredom reveals itself as energy—an energy that is part of the texture of our enlightened potential.

NCR: Shi-nè enables us to find ourselves beyond the suffocating frontiers of boredom. Shi-nè enables us to dissolve the tension of our anxiety within the infinite horizon of our being. This intimate dimension of being includes both the energy of wordless wonderment and the energy of boredom, as ornaments of its relaxed immensity.

KD: Once we develop our experience of shi-nè, boredom is no longer "boredom" but a wellspring of nourishment—a rolling wave of energy. So, from the point of view of shi-nè, boredom marks the beginning of realization. Without boredom there can be no possibility of discovery. If the experience of boredom is avoided, the opportunity of entering a new dimension of being is also avoided.

NCR: Boredom is one of the defense mechanisms of unenlightenment. It manifests whenever the suspicion arises that we are not as solid, permanent, separate, continuous, and defined as we thought we were.[7] Shi-nè is not concerned with contemplation.[8] No matter how profound a concept or point of view may be, no matter how deeply moving it may be, no matter to what spiritual elevation it takes us, "contemplation" is *not* the practice of shi-nè. Such conjecture or "cognitive dwelling" may well have great benefits. Such contemplation may inspire a "better" life, but this is not the direct function of shi-nè.

What, then, is this practice of shi-nè? Shi-nè is not prayer, relaxation, dreaming, drowsing, entrancement, directed or guided thinking,

7. The characteristics solid, permanent, separate, continuous, and defined relate to the hidden-agenda criteria that we use to substantiate our existence. These criteria are psychological aspects of the five psychophysical elements: earth, water, fire, air, and space. In Sutra these are explored in terms of the *skandhas*.
8. The word *contemplation* is sometimes used with reference to Dzogchen, but it is used in a specialized sense rather than the dictionary definition of considering or thinking about a topic.

contemplation, thoughtless blankness, introspection, or any other state that is not precisely and completely present. There is a Tibetan meditation adage that answers this question eloquently: "Meditation—*isn't*. Getting used to—*is*." It is said that meditation *isn't*, because it's not an end in itself. It is said that getting used to *is*, because the enlightened state is already there and we simply have to become accustomed to that. So, meditation is getting used to the enlightened state, cooperating with the enlightened state.

KD: What's important is *simply being*. We simply get used to the condition in which thoughts are not present or in which they arise and dissolve. Boredom is actually the threshold of discovery. You see, boredom is the official sign, complete with exclamation mark, that is erected by the petty tyrant of dualistic strategizing. It reads, "Do not under any circumstances proceed any further on pain of feeling nervous and ill at ease!" Many people will want to give up at that point. From a conventional perspective, who could blame them? But from the perspective of shi-nè, this is just the point at which something interesting could happen—if we simply continue to sit. If notice is taken of the sign and its imperative is obeyed, one would unavoidably stay within the boundaries of conditioning. But if the practice of shi-nè is pursued, one may well find oneself trespassing into unexplored territory. The method of shi-nè encourages us to question authority.

NCR: It transgresses the laws of fixed limitations. It infringes on the legislation of perceptual myopia. It violates the edicts of conceptual contrivance. It disobeys the rules of self-protectiveness. [*Khandro Déchen laughs*] Our sense of comfort is a dreadful dictator. Unenlightenment is strictly autocratic and, under such an authoritarian regime, there's no freedom or personal responsibility.

Q: You describe boredom as a defense mechanism that comes up when you suspect that you're not as solid, permanent, etc., as you thought you were. This sounds more like a fear reaction to me. Like,

"I'm not who I thought I was, and this is really quite scary." It would seem that it would take a certain momentum in order to break through this fear. How does one gather this sort of momentum?

NCR: Actually, I'd say that fear was a greater degree of openness in this case. It sounds as if you've already gone beyond boredom.

KD: Yes, boredom is a purposeful ignoring of what's going on around you, a shutting-down process. It's the opposite of the state of openness. To actually be open to fear in sitting is to have accomplished something with practice. I think it's useful to acknowledge that. It's very encouraging.

Q: You describe unenlightenment as an authoritarian regime where there's no freedom or personal responsibility. Why does one have to practice shi-nè in order to be personally responsible for making choices?

NCR: Because responsibility requires knowledge.

KD: If one is reacting according to preset patterns, then that's not really being responsible.

NCR: It becomes the same as the pleas at the Nuremberg trials: "I was only following orders." If we merely follow the rules of our conditioning, then there is no sense in which we are responding to real situations. We are simply applying the nearest rule to what is presenting itself.

Q: I have heard Dzogchen Sem-dé referred to as "the mental series." Could you say why that is?

NCR: That would be a misconception based upon translating the *sem* in Dzogchen Sem-dé as little-*m* mind, which, while accurate, is not actually what *sem* means in that context. The *sem* in Dzogchen Sem-dé is a contraction for *sem-nyid*, which means "the nature of Mind." It is also said to be a contraction of *changchub-sem*, or bodhicitta.

Q: Why bodhicitta, Rinpoche? Doesn't that mean compassion?

NCR: Sure—but again in the context of Dzogchen, the word *changchub-sem* is used to refer to the nature of Mind, so the term is synonymous with sem nyid.

Q: So you really have to approach all this from a fresh perspective.

NCR: Sure. I have a story about that . . . In 1994, when Kyabjé Chhi'mèd Rig'dzin Rinpoche visited our home in South Wales, we talked at length about the intrinsic mechanism of "comprehension" and "incomprehension." We were drinking tea at the time, and so Rinpoche used the most immediate analogy. He said: "Understanding is a special art—like receiving a bowl of tea. If your bowl is full, you can receive no more tea. To receive fresh tea, you must first drain or empty your bowl. Sometimes you must also clean your bowl, otherwise the stale residue of old tea will pollute the fresh tea. If you are with friends who have clean bowls but you do not have a clean bowl, what happens? They will say, 'This tea is very good!' They will be enjoying its taste. But if your bowl is dirty, you will not think it's so good. You would rather not drink it." So, yes . . . freshness is needed.

Q: You said that there was a misconception that meditation was a relaxation method, but that this isn't true of shi-nè. Can't shi-nè be relaxing even though it's not a relaxation technique?

KD: Yes . . . if we're discussing the result of shi-nè, but not necessarily if we're discussing the actual practice—especially in its initial phases. Until we arrive at the state of stable shi-nè, there is going to be some sense of struggle at the very least—some sense of frustration that this famous stable state is impossible to reach. And that doesn't precisely lend itself to relaxation.

NCR: This idea has arisen because some well-meaning people have put across the idea that "meditation" is a way of winding down after a tense or exhausting day in the fields, the office, hospital, shopping mall, abattoir, production line, oil rig, supermarket checkout, executive boardroom . . .

KD: . . . firing range, or wherever [*laughs*]. We feel that this view is mistaken. Buddhism isn't therapeutic in that sense. Confronting the conditioning that prevents true relaxation cannot be said to be relaxing. I think there's some difficulty here with regard to the use of the word *relaxation*. I feel that what most people think of as relaxation isn't relaxation according to the definition that exists in Dzogchen terminology. What is commonly understood as relaxation we would have to call partial relaxation, or relative relaxation . . . the mere sense of being at rest, or the temporary absence of obvious anxiety.

NCR: Dzogchen speaks of the total relaxation of everything into its own condition of primal purity. This isn't a state of rest or stasis, but a vibrant state of uninhibited interaction with reality.

CHAPTER 2

Thoughts and Clouds

The gomchenma *seems quite young—but appearance can be deceptive. You realize that you are unable to put even an approximate age to this person. She wears an undyed homespun* ngakma's *skirt and a sheepskin waistcoat. She wears an embroidered* gom-tag *across her chest—parallel bands of swirling clouds in blue, red, and white. Her conch earrings hide in her long, loose-hanging hair. A nine-eyed gZi stone hangs on a golden chain around her neck, but in all other respects she is utterly simple.*

*M*EDITATION—*isn't.* Getting used to—*is.* What subtle meaning could be hidden in such an odd grammatical construction? Before we elaborate on this theme, you will need to gain experience of practice. Once you have had a personal encounter with silent sitting, this kind of language will seem less foreign. It is invaluable at this point to sit, in order to become familiar with what practice signifies in terms of body, energy, and mind.

Parts one and two of this book are a handbook of the Four Naljors of Dzogchen Sem-dé, but they also include material to help those who are relatively new to Buddhism and the practice of silent sitting meditation. Shi-nè, as it is described within the Four Naljors, is a somewhat unapproachable subject for those with no knowledge of the terminology of nonduality. We have therefore provided a series of preliminary exercises that form a springboard into the *direct practice of emptiness.*

This manual needs to be approached one page at a time—one exercise at a time. Even if one has experience of practice, the following exercises may well prove interesting, stemming as they do from lesser-known yogic sources. This is a practical guide. It is therefore designed to be used in conjunction with practical exercises, geared to take one to the level of experience at which the later explanations become comprehensible. Reading ahead may be of no help, unless you have significant experience of silent sitting in a Buddhist tradition. If you do not have such experience, reading ahead may merely fuel preconceptions with regard to experiences before you have had the opportunity of discovering them for yourself. Reading ahead will preclude opportunities for gaining fresh experience—as distinct from preempted experience. We would therefore advise most people to begin with the first exercise, if only to participate in the flow of this manual. This is a matter not only of practicality, but of gaining a feel for the style of our explanation.

EXERCISE 1

Sit comfortably somewhere quiet. Sit with your eyelids comfortably drooping—almost closed, or partially open—just enough to let in a little light. Try to sit reasonably upright and in such a way that your body will not keep reminding you of its presence. If thoughts come, let them come. If thoughts go, let them go. If you find yourself involved in a stream of discursive thoughts, and you notice what is happening, do not be upset or annoyed—just let go of your involvement. Keep letting go of your involvement. Remain uninvolved.

Simply let go of whatever arises in your mind. Keep releasing your grasp on whatever you may have found yourself grasping. Simply let your mind be as it is. Continue letting your mind be as it is. Whatever happens, allow your mind to be as it is. Continue letting your mind be as it is. If you feel good, do not cling to the sensation or the thoughts that surround that feeling. If you feel bad, do not reject the sensation or the thoughts that surround that feeling. If you feel nothing at all, attempt not to drift into numbness and lack of presence. Attempt to remain alert, but without undue tension.

Try this for twenty minutes or so. See how it goes, but without any pressing expectation. If you have already gained some experience in practice and you are able to sit for longer, sit for as long as you would usually sit. If you are used to sitting with your eyes open, then continue in that practice and be open to whatever that experience becomes.

EXERCISE 1   FOLLOW-UP

If you have tried to follow the instructions in the first exercise, you will have made a good start. What you experienced was the play of your own energy. Whatever you thought or felt was useful. It provides you with valuable insights into how you see the world. The success of the exercise lies in remaining honest with yourself. Success is not dependent on having a "wonderful, peaceful experience"—after all, sleep is also peaceful. Success depends upon being honest and upon being prepared to experience yourself outside the context of your normal perceptual structures.

There is a time for the intellect and a time for letting it rest. The intellect functions perfectly within its own parameters, and the practice of sitting can show us the limitations of those parameters. In this way, view and meditation encourage each other. Maybe now it would be opportune to consider questions that may have been raised as a result of this exercise. Maybe you would like to repeat the first exercise, but if you do, avoid taking your questions with you. Put them aside. When we sit, we simply sit. When we question, we avoid trying to establish firm conclusions. Learning how to say "I don't know" is one of the most profound lessons we can learn. Try not to take the experience of silent sitting too seriously—it can often be quite amusing! Try the first exercise at least two or three times more before you proceed.

Exercise 2

Sit comfortably somewhere quiet. Sit with your eyelids comfortably drooping—almost closed, or partially open—just enough to let in a little light. Try to sit reasonably upright and in such a way that your body will not keep reminding you of its presence.

Whatever thoughts arise, block them. Cut them off immediately. Whatever thoughts are in your mind, force them out. Remain without thought. Continue to remain without thought.

Try this exercise for an hour. (If you already have considerable experience of silent sitting practice, try this exercise for longer—perhaps two or even three hours, but not longer than you would find comfortable.)

It is not necessary to remain physically still for this exercise.

Continue to the third exercise after what seems to you to be a comfortable rest.

Try to experience both exercises on the same day. The closer these two exercises are to each other, the better. Please engage in this exercise *before* reading the instructions for the third exercise. Reading the instructions for the next exercise will completely negate the value of this exercise.

Exercise 3

Sit very comfortably somewhere quiet with your eyes closed or partially open. Sit in an armchair if necessary in order to be as comfortable as possible and in order to sit for as long as possible.

Try to sit reasonably upright. Think continuously and actively about anything you like. Try not to allow any gaps at all between thoughts. If you become aware of the slightest gap in your thought process, fill it as quickly as possible and try to ensure that no further gaps occur. Fill your mind with as many thoughts as you can. Avoid investigating your visual surroundings as stimuli. Avoid going to sleep.

Try this for at least an hour and a half to two hours. If you are

already experienced with silent sitting practice and are used to remaining still for long periods of time, try this exercise for at least
three hours—longer, if possible.

EXERCISES 2 AND 3   EXPERIENTIAL ACCOUNTS

Now you have had two very different experiences. Observe the
way in which they were different and the way in which they may
have been similar. A valuable lesson has been learned, but what do
you think it is?

Write a commentary on the experiences of exercises 2 and 3
before continuing to read this chapter. Then review those com-
mentaries after reading about the origin of the second and third
exercises.

THE ORIGINS OF EXERCISES 2 AND 3

In Tibet, prior to the middle of the last century, there were different types of spiritual practitioners. There were the monks and
nuns who lived mainly in their respective gompas.[1] When most
people consider Tibet, it is the monastic orders that usually spring
to mind. Monasticism is the dominant religious culture associated
with Tibetan Buddhism, but it is not the only one. There was another major spiritual tradition that was available to both men and
women—the noncelibate sangha of Vajrayana. These men and
women were the *ngakpa*s and *ngakma*s who existed within every
stratum of Tibetan society.[2] They lived in *dratsang*s (colleges) and
small rural communities. They lived in nomadic encampments
called *gar*s, but many were wanderers. There were gCodpas and

---

1. "Meditation place," usually translated as monastery.
2. sNgags pa (male) and sNgags ma or sNgags mo (female) are ordained members of the
noncelibate, nonmonastic Tantric community called the gö-kar-chang-lo'i dé (gos
dKar lCang lo'i sDe), "white skirt long hair series" or ngak'phang (sNgags 'phang),
mantra-wielding sangha.

gCodmas[3] who roamed from place to place with little else but a bell, a thigh-bone trumpet, and the large gCod drum, whose slow, resonant heartbeat choreographed the energy of their practice. Some were recluses who lived high in the mountains. Many of these were répas or rémas, who wore either simple, lightweight white cotton robes or nothing at all.[4] In the tradition of their practice of *tu-mo*, the spatial heat yoga, it is customary only to wear white cotton.

Some ngakpas and ngakmas were married householders, and some were people who spent most of their lives in retreat. Many of these Lamas were profound Tantric masters surrounded by groups of disciples who lived at a discreet distance, absorbed in the practices their teacher had set for them. The mountain retreat places used by these Lamas and their students were usually built as structures that made use of preexisting caves. Some were simple and provided little shelter from the wind and snow, but some were quite comfortable. Some caves were more like small houses, with wooden flooring, windows, and sometimes more than one room. They were ideal places to spend many weeks, months, or years in retreat.

Access to these places was usually quite difficult, and food supplies sometimes ran out, but such was the life of a *gomchen* or *gomchenma*.[5] It certainly was not the easiest of lives, but these Lamas often had spectacular powers that enabled them to endure all kinds of privations. The fame of such Lamas often inspired those with mystic leanings to seek instruction from them—whatever the cost in terms of loss of conventional comforts.

Now let us suppose that you are such a person. Let us imagine that you feel drawn to enter fully into spiritual life and that you

3. Practitioners of gCod (pronounced *chöd*), the method of cutting attachment to the corporeal form as a reference point that validates existence as solid, permanent, separate, continuous, and defined.

4. *Réma* (ras ma) is the female form of the word *répa* (ras pa), as in Milarépa (mi la ras pa). Kyungchen Aro Lingma was called Jétsunma Khandro Yeshé Réma prior to her discovery of the Aro gTér, a cycle of pure vision revelation teachings.

5. Great master of meditation.

wish to approach such a Lama. We will paint a picture of what it might have been like to have met with such a person—and from that you may well discover more about the two exercises you just experienced.

Imagine that you are living in Tibet—a high alpine land cut off from the rest of the world. Here there is only one great goal in life, so unless you try for lesser goals such as wealth or mundane power, the spiritual goal stands alone. The situation is not as clearcut in the West, or in contemporary society almost anywhere on the globe. Since you have read this far, we presume you must share a similar degree of enthusiasm about this unique goal. It will therefore not be hard for you to imagine a situation in which your choices would be far simpler.

You have heard much concerning the Lamas who live in the mountains close to your home. For years now you have felt restless. You have become dissatisfied with the repetitive rhythms of religious observance, to which you have been accustomed since childhood. You have the idea in your mind of setting out on a serious quest. You want to find out what would be possible if you could enter into practice under the guidance of an accomplished master in the mountains. This was not an unusual undertaking in Tibet. So, after looking carefully at your life, you decide to visit the *tsi-pa* and *mo-pa*.[6] You have had some dreams that seem auspicious. Various omens have indicated that this is the time for change. The mo-pa gives the prognosis that your plan will go well but that it will not be without difficulty. The tsi-pa gives you a good day to set out and suggests rites that should be performed on your behalf.

So you seek an audience with the abbot of the local monastery—he is noted for his clairvoyance. You ask for advice as to where you should go. He looks at you with a smile and asks a few questions about what your practice has been. You explain the practices in which you have been engaged, and he seems satisfied that your in-

---

6. Astrologer and diviner.

tentions are appropriate. He gives you directions, various indications, and a blessing for your journey.

When the day arrives, you set out to seek the meditation master. The journey into the mountains is long and difficult. You take shelter where you can—usually under a tree, wrapped in your *chuba* coat and blanket. Maybe for the first time you are able just to lie and look up at the stars. Your small campfire keeps you warm. Somehow everything seems delightful—apart, that is, from the uncertainty in your mind as to how you will be received. The abbot has given you no assurances that the reclusive Lama will accept you. You have heard that being accepted as a disciple of one of these gomchens is not necessarily an easy matter. You have heard that the method of such Lamas is to welcome some aspirants yet turn others away without a word of explanation. There are some reclusive masters who throw stones at visitors from a distance, so they do not even get close enough to pay their respects. Some of these gomchens are known to be crazy wisdom masters, and they can behave in almost any way.

There is one thing, however, of which you are quite sure—such masters hold teachings that lead to swift realization. The swift path is said to be strenuous, difficult, and sometimes dangerous. That is well known to you. Sometimes such Lamas make extraordinary demands on their disciples. The history of Marpa and Milarépa, at least in its rudimentary form, is known to all Tibetans—so, with a mixture of excitement and trepidation, you ponder what might await you. You wonder how you will cope with the experiences that lie ahead—after all, the mo-pa did forewarn you of certain difficulties. Maybe you will find that you are not a suitable candidate for a gomchen's teachings. Maybe you will be sent away as a failure—unable either to pursue your desire or to return to the life you once led. What if you fail? You might never be able to settle upon anything—always torn between what could have been and that to which you would have to resign yourself. Your thoughts race with the stories you have heard. You are so stirred with imaginings that you almost tingle with apprehension.

It is a bewildering experience. Somehow it seems to have become a great adventure, even in the traveling, and there are many miles yet to tread.

Finally, after several weeks, you approach the end of the last valley. You begin to climb upward, closer to the feet of the snowy peaks. Soon you find yourself among spectacular ragged mountains. The track becomes an obstacle course—strewn with rocks and stones and cut by cascading rivulets of mountain meltwater. It is wonderful simply to be among the mountains beyond the dog dung and noise of the town. Your spirits lift as you climb higher— but suddenly you hear a yell that arrests your step. It is quite far off, but nevertheless, it makes your scalp tingle. You walk carefully. You have heard tell of bears and wolves and *mi-ma-yin*—nonhuman entities. You have also heard of the *mi-gö*, the yeti, which has a high-pitched shriek.

Looking into the distance you begin to see, or imagine you see, the tiny forms of people. They sit in the distance among rocks on the higher slopes of a remote valley. As you make your way closer you are able to pick out a few men and women practicing physical exercises in the open air. You have never observed movements of this type before, and you become fascinated by the spectacle. Is it these people who emitted the piercing yells that made you fear the mi-gö?

All at once you notice him. He sits a short distance away and appears almost as if he is waiting for you. Your approach has been observed. You are greeted with an unaffected, good-natured smile from a strange-looking person. He has long tousled hair coiled into an immense nestlike structure on his head. The remains of his monastic robes are bleached pink by the sun and copiously patched. He lifts himself to his feet in one graceful, seamless movement and measures the distance between you in slow, almost insolent strides. You feel slightly more timid than you would have expected to feel, but somehow you know there is no problem in this confrontation. The young man now gazing at you has a remarkable *presence*. Apart from his wild appearance, he looks fresh and bright—unnervingly

37

awake. He takes in each detail of what you are, quite exactly, but without any sense of caution or suspicion. He notices each movement you make, each intonation of your voice. You feel that it would not be possible to hide anything from a person like this—even if you had the inclination. "Maybe he's the gomchen," you wonder, but no. He laughs at the idea, but in a kindly way, so as not to make you feel foolish or embarrassed. He tells you that the gomchenma, for this Lama is a woman, has been expecting you for some weeks. You are to follow him to his cave where you will be able to refresh yourself.

The other disciples all have more or less the same quality of being. They all laugh quite frequently—often unusually loudly. They laugh at almost anything: the sun striking out from behind a cloud, the way in which a marmot suddenly sits up or a goat belches. Their sense of humor is a little disorienting, but somehow infectious. It has a way of putting you at your ease. The disciples practice and work—some fetch wood, some carry water, and some cook. They take care with whatever they are doing, and the sounds of awareness spells are often on their lips. Some are in retreat; they have food brought to them. Some are returning from journeys into the mountains to collect herbs for medicinal purposes. Some are setting off to visit powerful places for practice. Others are preparing to enter retreat. They all seem to have a singular brightness in their eyes—their gaze is unblinking yet unstrained. You ask questions, but not many answers are forthcoming. Some things, you are informed, will have to wait until your meeting with the gomchenma. You have never before met people like this, and your customary modes of responding seem meaningless. You wonder what the gomchenma can be like when her disciples are so extraordinary—so perceptive, immediate, and carefree.

Finally the day arrives. Your presence is requested by the Lama. How will she seem? Lamas can be gentle, severe, irascible, or wrathful. They can be hilarious, wry, serious, or solemn, garrulous, impassive, inscrutable, or aloof. They can be handsomely dressed, simply clad, or ragged. You wonder about her, because her disciples have given nothing away.

When you finally meet the Lama, she eludes most of the human possibilities you have pondered yet contains many of them in an inexplicable pattern that is never quite definable. The gomchenma seems quite young—but appearance can be deceptive. You realize that you are unable to put even an approximate age to this person. She wears an undyed homespun ngakma's skirt and a sheepskin waistcoat. She wears an embroidered *gom-tag*[7] across her chest—parallel bands of swirling clouds in blue, red, and white. Her conch earrings hide in her long, loose-hanging hair. A nine eyed *gZi* stone[8] hangs on a golden chain around her neck, but in all other respects she is utterly simple.

There is a young child sitting in her cave who gazes at you in a slightly unnerving manner. You are not quite sure whether you are looking at a boy or a girl—the features that greet you could belong to either. He is the gomchenma's son, and he sits on a large tiger skin.[9] Once he has inspected you, he returns to playing with some small pebbles of various colors, which he seems to be arranging in groups as if it were a game. You wonder if this might be a form of *mo* because of the seriousness with which the young child is playing. You are not certain what to say to the gomchenma, but she greets you with a warm smile. She waves aside your attempt at prostrations, which are the usual formal greeting to a Lama. She looks at you intently but says nothing for a long time. Then she

7. Meditation strap used in the practice of Dzogchen Long-dé, usually constructed as three bands of fabric of the yogic colors—blue, red, and white.
8. gZi stones (pronounced *zee*) are special stones found in Tibet. They have "water eyes," circles that appear in patterns along with patterns of lines. gZi are naturally occurring, and there are a variety of mysterious accounts of what their origin may have been. Basically, they are archeological finds that originate in Tibet and the Himalayan region. They are currently classified as agate, and the general opinion seems to be that the markings are made by applying a bleaching agent in the form of paste and subjecting the stones to high temperatures.
9. Tiger skins are connected very much with practices of the wrathful awareness-beings, especially Dorje Tröllö and Tsogyel Tröllö.

laughs. She already seems to know all about you, either from clarity or from what she has been told by her disciples. You understand somehow that this is not the time for questions. She has instructions to give you, and they are fairly cryptic: "Tomorrow, go to the cave below the outcrop of rock shaped like a vulture's beak. Sit from dawn to dusk and have no thoughts. You may use any method you wish to banish thought from your mind. When the day is over, return to me with word of your experiences." She smiles again. You are not sure why, but it seems that the smile betokens that it is time for you to go. She gives you a blessing, and you leave. While you were with the Lama in her cave, it seemed as if you had been in there for days, but when you leave, it seems as if it had been only seconds. You feel slightly disoriented. This has been the strangest meeting of your life.

You ask her disciples about the instructions you have been given, but as far as they are concerned this is something private between you and their Lama—Khandro Rinpoche, as the gom-chenma is known. They do not wish to hear about it or to comment. They do, however, confirm that Khandro Rinpoche seems to have accepted you as a disciple. They seem genuinely pleased by this, which is encouraging, but they are prepared to say nothing further—no matter how much you request what you consider to be necessary information. So far, nothing has taken place that resembles anything you had previously imagined. This is somehow disappointing, yet somehow more intriguing than you had expected. Once accepted as a disciple, one can expect anything to happen. Lamas such as Khandro Rinpoche can be highly unorthodox in their teaching methods, and there are no reference points against which one can check.

As the next day dawns, you go to the cave below the vulture's beak crag and adopt the meditation posture. You make yourself comfortable. You wait for your thoughts to settle. You have some conjecture that if you merely sit long enough, it will happen. But nothing happens beyond the usual stream of conceptuality. Previously you had chanted and visualized, and the thoughts that came and went seemed somehow less problematic. But now, instead of being able to rest in a peaceful quietude, *everything* begins to happen! Your mind is crowded with thought! Panic begins to rise at the idea of not succeeding in fulfilling Khandro Rinpoche's instruction. You try to force thoughts out of your mind. You tense yourself. You try to will your thoughts away, but *that* just becomes another thought! You even shout, "Go away!" and clap your hands as if dispelling demons, but the words merely echo in the cave, and further thoughts create a counterpoint to the echoes in your mind-stream. You shake your head. You hold your breath. You shake your head again. Nothing works. Your mind is filled with the wish to eliminate thought, but there is no hope of abolishing *that* thought. It is paradoxical and completely frustrating. You have never known such a continuous bombardment of thought.

Dusk descends and the day finally comes to an end. You climb the track miserably, dispirited by failure. You fear Khandro Rinpoche's response to your pathetic attempt to follow the *togden's* path.[10] You wonder whether you will be dismissed as unfit for teaching or even gathering yak dung; but no, Khandro Rinpoche bursts out laughing. She is highly amused by the tale of your mental and physical antics. Her son is also amused. "Good! Excellent!" She looks at you in a kindly way and says, "You have made a good attempt. You have done well! Tomorrow go back to the cave and sit from dawn till dusk again—but this time have nothing but thought without interruption. Think of anything at all, all day long—but allow no gaps to occur between thoughts." Naturally, you are well pleased—even though you have no understanding of why you were seen to have done well. You take your leave of Khandro Rinpoche, thinking, "Well that will be easy, I am bound to succeed at that if today was anything by which to judge. I seem to be brimming with thought most of the time quite naturally and without the slightest effort!"

10. Togdens are yogic ngak'phang practitioners, usually either nomadic or living in caves, who wear their hair in a characteristic matted style piled on top of their heads.

So the next day at dawn you go back to the cave with some sense of confidence. But after a while you discover that your new instructions are no less impossible than those you had previously received. Nothing is occurring in the manner in which you imagined it would. You start out having several pleasant subjects spring to mind. You think about them. You make various speculations and follow them through, but after a while the process begins to lose its savor. Your imagination shows signs of flagging, and you even begin to get a bit bored by the process. You wonder where your delight in pondering has gone. You used to be able to let your mind drift from subject to subject, but somehow the pleasure you took in that process seems flat and uninspired. You remember being able to daydream, but in this cave you begin to notice the fabric of thoughts becoming patchy. The things in which you invested so much mental energy no longer seem so absorbing. You try to infuse these stray-dog ideas with new life, but it does not work particularly well. Most subjects you attempt to dwell upon seem unusually hollow and lacking in meaning. Your practice begins to become unsettling when the most significant aspects of your life cease to hold your attention for long. You root around desperately for a new subject to consider. You attempt to generate new perspectives on old issues—but this scheme fails as all the previous schemes have failed. You feel you would love to walk in the mountains and explore the area. It would be far easier to think if you were walking in the freedom of the outside world. But you have to sit in a cave. As comfortable as the cave is, it is as lacking in actual romance as the village you left weeks before. This is the new and exciting life of yogic practice . . . What is left? Maybe you attempt to conjure up sexual fantasies—they used to voluptuate into your mind so easily. But now your imagination does not seem able to produce anything sufficiently interesting or provocative to stimulate you. Every attempt at entertainment disintegrates into a vague tedium in which thought comes to a halt.

Eventually you get to the point where gaps in the thought process become impossible to avoid. Long before the day is over you have to jerk yourself out of longer and longer periods of blankness. You feel wretched, having failed again. You cannot even do what once came so easily to you, and you are sure that Khandro Rinpoche will send you away to try elsewhere.

When you tell her your story, however, she looks pleased. She nods her head and smiles as you relate your tale of woe, and when you have finished, she bursts out laughing again. She congratulates you: "Good! Wonderful! Now you know how to practice perfectly!"

You are completely bewildered by this. You think, "What can this mean? I am more confused now than when I first arrived! This makes no sense to me." You wonder whether Khandro Rinpoche is simply testing you with impossible procedures, but she has actually given you exemplary instructions. You have learned the most valuable lesson in the best possible way. It is a lesson that you will never forget. Something inside you tells you that all is not quite as it seems. You begin to find the situation slightly amusing. Khandro Rinpoche is laughing. You are also laughing—but when the hilarity has passed, Khandro Rinpoche explains in a sentence exactly what it is that you have learned.

The conclusion of the story we have just recounted may sound odd to those who are familiar with Western educational procedures, but within this field of instruction, someone else is often needed to focus our experience. All the elements of understanding have been brought together, and they exist within us. We simply lack the ability to comprehend the understanding that is waiting to be experienced. The disciple in our story had no idea why the gomchenma was laughing, no idea why she was pleased by her student's apparent failure, and no idea what could possibly have been learned from those experiences.

Sometimes, if one has had the right experiences and one is in the right place at the right time with the right person, a few words will change one's life. This is a singularly efficacious method of teaching. When Khandro Rinpoche taught her student in the manner described, she was equipping her disciple with the necessary experiences to understand exactly what she was going to convey in relation to shi-nè. It is a powerful moment when one realizes, "I have known this without knowing it! It is so simple!"

In order for us to understand anything in the fullest sense, the circumstances have to be appropriate. In the right circumstances, a few words will pull together what appeared to be a jumble of disparate strands of information. What seemed at first to be confusion was in fact the basis for a remarkable understanding. It comes as a significant insight to realize that we can be learning—without even knowing what is taking place. To work with a Lama is of inestimable value, and we hope that this book encourages you to find such a person.

In our story, Khandro Rinpoche was teaching her disciple several vital points with regard to the mind:

- One cannot force the mind.
- Attempting to force thought out merely results in the proliferation of thought.
- Attempting to force thought to be continuous merely results in the disintegration of the thought flow.

When she said to her disciple, "Good! Wonderful! Now you know how to practice perfectly," she meant that her disciple had the knowledge that it was useless to try to force the mind.

- To practice perfectly is to proceed without force.
- If we attempt to force thought out—the mind rebels.
- If we try to force thought to be continuous—the mind rebels.

This is why in the practice of shi-nè we *let go and let be.* We do not encourage thought, yet neither do we block it. We treat the process of thought gently. We let thoughts come, and we let thoughts go. We translate shi-nè as "remaining uninvolved." If thoughts arise, one lets them arise; if they dissolve, one allows their dissolution. If thoughts are present, one allows their presence. One does not add to them or protract them. If thoughts depart, one does not detain them. One treats them as welcome yet transient guests. One treats thought as a fire that has served its purpose—one merely ceases to add further fuel. If one stops fueling thought with active involvement, thought settles and one enters into a calm and undisturbed state.

The exercises we have introduced are far shorter than the dawn-till-dusk exercises portrayed in the story of Khandro Rinpoche and her disciple. It is not possible to re-create the environment in which such teaching methods were possible, and so we have not attempted it. But it is possible to gain some idea from experimenting with these exercises even for short periods. Anyone who attempts to force thought will come to *know* that if one wishes to work with attachment to the thought process, one must employ some method other than coercion.

This brings us back to the Tibetan adage: Meditation *isn't*; getting used to *is*. When it is said that meditation *isn't*, what is signified is that meditation is not a method of *doing*. It is a method of *not-doing*. One does not involve oneself in doing anything. One does not instigate anything or impose anything. One does not add anything or elaborate anything. One simply remains. One simply maintains presence in motiveless observation.

When it is said that getting used to *is*, what is signified is a practice in which one is simply getting used to *being*. One acclimatizes oneself to the undefined dimension of existence. We are unused to our own enlightenment, so meditation is a way of "getting used to" it. In terms of deep-rooted attachment to thought, one is getting used to nonreferentiality. One is getting used to being referenceless.[11]

The approach we take in this book is similar to the method of the gomchenma—we first introduce method and then follow that with

11. Those who have some experience of shi-nè, shamatha, vipashyana, or zazen and find themselves wishing to explore what is meant by "being referenceless" should see chapter 7. We would recommend, however, that whatever your experience of sitting, it would be helpful not to skip this initial material altogether because you may well find something new in it due to the nature of the approach being adopted.

explanation. This means that by the time the explanation (or theory) is given, it should make experiential sense. We will therefore begin with basic methods of shi-nè. Methods of shi-nè differ, depending upon their origin within different Buddhist systems. As explained previously, the method of shi-nè given here relates to the Four Naljors— the ngöndro, or preliminary practices, of Dzogchen Sem-dé, the series of the nature of Mind. In order to gain a thorough grounding, practicing all the given exercises is recommended—whatever your previous experience.

It is crucial to know quite personally that meditation *isn't*, and that getting used to *is*.

CHAPTER 3

Presence and Awareness

Imagination relies on empty perception. Painting relies on empty planes. Sculpture relies on empty space. Music relies on empty time. Literature relies on empty concepts. If we are to realize the art of freedom, if we are to discover our creative potential, we need to rely on the experience of our intrinsic vibrant emptiness—the beginningless ground of what we are.

WHEN WE ENTER into the dimension of the Four Naljors, we come face to face with the raw dynamic of ourselves. It is an experience of tremendous space and ordinariness, but one that is not necessarily comfortable. In shi-nè, committed practitioners are obliged to confront difficult feelings as workable. It is a method in which practitioners discover aspects of themselves with which they may not be entirely happy. If we can relax, however, and allow the situation of sitting to be as it is, we can begin to develop a new tolerance for the entirety of our human situation. Accepting ourselves *as we are* is the only position from which we can proceed to act or to understand anything. Shi-nè is no exception to this principle.

This is the embarkation point. Everything we discover when we sit is what we are in that moment. What we may discover when we commence to sit is that there exists a conceptual cargo we have "decided" to carry. Having sat for a certain length of time, we will know: "*This*—in this moment—is what I happen to be." This will never be terrible. There will be nothing lurking in our "depths" that could possibly cause devastating dismay. As practitioners, we will have dropped the twenty-four-hour floor show of entertainments that caused us personal estrangement. Once we have sat through the theatrical performance of attempting to hide from ourselves, there will be nothing left to cause distress. The only problem is that this could take longer than we might like.

The process of opening to the fact of how we happen to be can take days, weeks, months, or maybe even years. We each have our individual capacity for realization and our individual obstacles. We each have our own histories of experience on which to draw. Sitting through the range of our unacknowledged negative feelings provides the experiential ballast necessary to become solid and grounded as a person. By "solid and grounded," we do not mean stolid and lumbering, in the style of a person with limited perceptual horizons. We simply mean someone who no longer daydreams while his or her dinner burns.

One could be solid and grounded in terms of one's imagination, in linking it to the practicality of how one could manifest creativity in the real world. To be an authentic artist, one actually has to produce something and accept the challenges of manifesting one's imagination, even if it proves inconvenient or pushes one's skills to the outer limit. This could be described as the first attainment: being able to acknowledge the range of permutations that comprise our response to existence.

Initially, the practice of shi-nè is *getting used to* the fact of our existence. We are here, and there is a texture that relates with that. It is a complete texture, containing both pleasure and pain, hope and fear, gain and loss, meeting and parting, pride and humiliation. Shi-nè provides the prime evidence of the texture of what we are—and there is no escaping the self-existent verdict of that. In the solitary confinement cell of shi-nè, fantasies and illusions die of hunger simply because they are no longer fed by the energy of our involvement with them.[1]

---

1. This does not mean that the creative artistic impulse is antithetical to the practice of shi-nè.

Imagination relies on empty perception. Painting relies on empty planes. Sculpture relies on empty space. Music relies on empty time. Literature relies on empty concepts. If we are to realize the art of freedom, if we are to discover our creative potential, we need to rely on the experience of our intrinsic vibrant emptiness—the beginningless ground of what we are.

The gateway to the art of freedom is the practice of shi-nè—our method of approaching the white canvas of Mind. With shi-nè we disengage from the process of imagination and fantasy of any kind— that is the nature of the practice. We are being completely non-manipulative and uninfluenced by anything. Working with active imagination or envisionment comes later, when we have connected more with the spaciousness of being.[2]

The experience of shi-nè may be uncomfortable. When we sit according to the instruction of the Four Naljors, we locate ourselves precisely in time and space. It may be an experience we would prefer to avoid rather than feel the possible rawness and vulnerability of being experientially pinpointed. We know, in a certain sense, that we have limited our options. We know that while practicing shi-nè we are where we are—just where we sit. We know that this is where we are going to be for as long as we have decided to sit. The world of our activity has stopped. The passage of time through which we had been traveling is without record of our active involvement. At one moment a film is running—an epic, a thriller, a comedy, or a melodrama. Then—suddenly—it freezes on a frame of an "I," sitting in a room attempting to exist. Suddenly there is no movement to distract from this alternately concrete and amorphous image. Every detail of this "I" is both there and not there at the same time. It can be disconcerting if we have never experienced ourselves as illusory before.

If we avoid shi-nè, we avoid direct confrontation with ourselves. But the painful patterns of frustration, which seem to fabricate themselves in life as circumstances dictate, exist whether we acknowledge

2. Envisionment or visualization is the practice of *internal seeing* in which one identifies with symbolic foci of realization.

them or not. It would appear that if we practice shi-nè, *we* begin to live our lives. If we do not practice shi-nè, *our lives* continue to live us. In some ways, shi-nè is the moment the shutter is released. The shutter mechanism exposes the film to reflected light, and that moment is the picture we acquire. That is who we are, at that moment—which is also a "momentless moment." Maybe we like it. Maybe we dislike it. Whichever it is, it is how we are. It is *as we are*—whether we like it, we dislike it, or we're indifferent to it.

When we practice shi-nè, we experience ourselves within a limited yet spatially unlimited point in time. We can attempt to obliterate that point in time by mentally reliving the past. We can attempt to obliterate that point in time by projecting possible future events. We can attempt to obliterate that point in time by sinking into an oblivious drowse. But we can also sit and *be what we are* in the moment. We can sit and aimlessly observe the present mind-moment arising from the death of the previous mind-moment. We can both exist and cease to exist at the same time.

This picture of shi-nè could be terrifically bleak in comparison to spiritually materialistic notions of "positivistic meaningfulness," but somehow shi-nè opens us to a wider sense of our humanity. We can discover that there is a greater meaning to be found in sheer *presence* than in the naïve affirmations of existence that pose as hope. The Buddhism of all schools begins with the hopelessness of dualism. Before we open ourselves to the hopelessness of our own strategies, an explosion that shatters the parameters of hope and fear is inconceivable.

QUESTIONS AND ANSWERS

QUESTION: I'm sorry about this question, but in terms of letting go of fantasies, I was thinking, at one level, that fantasy can be fun . . . and I was wondering how such an idea looks from your perspective.

NGAKPA CHÖGYAM RINPOCHE: [*laughs*] Yes. At one level I doubt whether Khandro Déchen or I would disagree. There's no reason to be sorry for the question, however—it's actually quite useful to look at this idea. We wouldn't like anyone to get the idea that imagination isn't kosher or something [*laughs*]. That would be somewhat grim.

KHANDRO DÉCHEN: [*laughs*] That may well be shocking in religious terms, especially for those who have already become involved with the practice of meditation in a Buddhist tradition. Generally, one is instructed to let go of "fantasy" in order to find "reality."

NCR: Within the divisionlessness of the nature of Mind, however, concepts of fantasy and reality have no meaning. They're simply the energy of Mind.

KD: We don't say this in order to advocate fantasy, but rather because anything that leans toward purism or Puritanism is not conducive to the experience of practice within the Four Naljors. Imagination is only a problem if one continually indulges in it as an escape from being present. Imagination can be either active or passive. Passive imagination is daydreaming. Daydreaming is a state in which one is not present—not even in the daydream. This is a drowsy, vague state of being that scarcely leaves a memory of the daydream. Active imagination, however, is a state in which one is present.

NCR: Yes. This is a creative capacity that can be used as a resource for self-healing, visionary discovery, and artistic creativity. Buddhism is not anti-art, and shi-nè is not anti-imagination—it's more a question of the relationship one has with one's imagination. If one is employing one's imagination as a means of establishing reference points. . . .

Q: Do you think that the intensity of this whole process of "sitting through the range of our unacknowledged negative feelings" can be too overwhelming for some people?

KD: Certainly. For some people, we really wouldn't recommend silent sitting at all. If people are at a stage of development where they're in need of psychotherapy, then they should always be cautious of spiritual practices that threaten the personality structure. When someone's sense of self-worth is extremely low, the experience of protracted periods of shi-nè could well be too overwhelming. It could be especially harmful for people at low levels of psychological health.

NCR: I'd say that involvement with spiritual practice and teachers, especially at the level of Tantra or Dzogchen, should really be avoided by people at low levels of psychological health. Unfortunately, people with interpersonally dysfunctional personalities are often drawn to this type of spiritual tradition, and such people would be very resentful if they were presented with such definitions of themselves.

CHAPTER 4

Nakedness and Perception

The discovery of shi-nè confronts us with the fact that our fear of nonexistence is both the driving force of duality and the sparkling-through of our beginningless enlightenment. So we are actually quite justified in mistrusting the nature of what we are, but that mistrust is usually aimed in the wrong direction. We mistrust the open dimension of being, rather than feeling suspicious of the conceptual criteria by which we habitually validate our existence. Through the practice of shi-nè we discover that our definitions are a barrier.

RIGPA[1] IS THE STATE of naked perception.[2] It is a naked flame that burns without consuming itself. It is naked in the sense that a sword is described as naked when it is unsheathed—when its blade glitters in the sunlight. Rigpa is the state of pure and total presence, stripped of referential clinging. The illusion of duality is self-

---

1. Rigpa (rig pa) is a term that has a particular meaning in the Dzogchen teachings. In the other Buddhist vehicles, it is employed to mean "knowledge" in the general sense of "knowing about." In Dzogchen, rigpa is a term for the nondual state that is realized through methods of "instantaneous presence."
2. chèr-thong (gCer mThong), naked perception.

divested through bare attention, and the essential reality of what we are exposes itself *as it is*.[3]

We mistrust the nature of what we are. We seem to need constant confirmation that we are actually here. We continually engage in the activity of seeking assurances of our existence. This is our penchant for unnecessarily clothing our naked awareness in concepts.[4] Mistrust of our own existence is our primary dualistic fixation, but it's a veiled mistrust that disguises itself as obduracy, irritation, obsessiveness, suspicion, and depression. This mistrust of existence sets the scene for us to manufacture our struggle with the world. Once the struggle is underway, we struggle with the outcome of that struggle in order to maintain the activity of struggling. Unless we practice silent sitting, we never meet this kind of mistrust face to face. And if we never apprehend this experiential mistrust, the explanations presented in the following chapters will not make a great deal of sense. So it is important to arrive at this level of understanding through our own experience of practice. Because we mistrust our existence, we scan our experience of being for "proofs of being" that are concretely viable. From this perspective, shi-nè is a disappointment because it does not generate the types of confirmations we want. So our inclination is to avoid practices such as shi-nè.

We shall repeat what we have explained in the preceding paragraph, but we shall turn the argument back to front to provide some experientially based reasoning: If we practice shi-nè and find ourselves within the gap that arises between thoughts, the inclination is to fill such gaps with conceptual material in order to feel comfortable. We try to either grab the experience of the gap, to retreat from the gap, or to retract *presence* from the gap. We are either attracted, averse, or indifferent. But whichever the reaction, the end result is the same—we fill the gap. We mask out the absence of thought. Whether we self-reference "positively," "negatively," or through the oblivion of

---

3. "As it is" is the literal translation of the word *chö* (chos, Skt. dharma).
4. rigpa chèrbu (rig pa gCer bu), naked awareness.

neutrality, we obliterate the gap with concept. We fill it with concepts of acceptance or rejection—or we drift into unconscious oblivion. The tendency is to do anything rather than remain present in the openness of what we are. We habitually fill gaps of any kind, because they contain no confirmation of our existence—we have no trust in being. Being is both thought and absence of thought, phenomena and emptiness, pattern and chaos. But when we begin to practice shi-nè, it soon becomes obvious that we are not comfortable with so vague a definition.

This is how it is when anyone begins to sit. All one has to do, if one has any doubt about this, is to practice shi-nè and find out. This goes for any part of our explanation—if you are not convinced, just sit and find out for yourself. Once you have practiced in this way, you will know that you are attached to the process of thinking and that you experience gaps as both difficult to find and difficult when *that* is where you *find yourself.*

The experience of sitting and doing nothing is also difficult because when we are not engaging in any specifically recognizable activity we lack the usual definitions. Simply sitting means that all we have left to prove that we exist is bodily presence and thought processes. If we get used to the physical dimension of sitting, then thought processes will be all we have left with which to define existence. Shi-nè puts those processes under the magnifying glass of nondiscursive observation, and a somewhat shocking learning process begins to take place. One learns that one would rather think about anything, no matter how banal, than let go of the thought process. It would seem as if thought is a need of some kind. Anyone spending more than two or three hours in a sensory deprivation chamber would be brought face to face with the nature of these "needs." One would be confronted with feelings of insubstantiality, fear, loneliness, paranoia, and bewilderment. One would also find out exactly what one wanted to do in reaction to such feelings. One would want to consolidate one's sense of identity, instigate specific defense activities, generate familiar trains of thought (and make contact with external objects), devise escape strategies (and complicated contingency plans), or—failing all else—attempt to fall asleep. One would discover that the space of absence in which one has found oneself fails to provide the sense of solidity, unchangeability, individuation, control, or definition that one usually requires in order to feel coherent.

The experience of total sensory deprivation could be extremely valuable to anyone who wanted to experience the reality of what is expressed here, but it is not a state that is easily available to most people. Shi-nè is a slower and less traumatic method of learning everything one could learn in a sensory deprivation chamber. The practice of shi-nè allows one to make discoveries in one's own time, and at a pace that allows the assimilation and integration of discoveries with one's everyday perceptual context. Shi-nè practice will show soon enough that one's dualistic system of self-referential proofs runs as follows: "In order to exist, I have to know all the time that I exist. In order to be convinced of that knowledge, I need constant proof of my existence in terms of finding myself to be solid, permanent, separate, continuous, and defined." The discovery of shi-nè confronts us with the fact that our fear of nonexistence is both the driving force of duality and the sparkling-through of our beginningless enlightenment. So we are actually quite justified in mistrusting the nature of what we are, but that mistrust is usually aimed in the wrong direction. We mistrust the open dimension of being rather than feeling suspicious of the conceptual criteria by which we habitually validate our existence. Through the practice of shi-nè, we discover that our definitions are a barrier. We discover that this barrier is built of feelings of insubstantiality, fear, isolation, agitation, and phlegmatic tedium. The practice of shi-nè is a provocative irritant to each one of the feelings. Life also irritates each—but not as definitively. So as long as we insist on maintaining fixed definitions of what we are, both shi-nè and our life experience will appear to promote dualistic discomfort and dualistic remedies for the same. The dualistic rationale continually seeks out definitions, so in a sense shi-nè is a way of relaxing out of that struggle.

The nature of existence continually helps and hinders the search for definitions in a completely impartial manner. The problem is that we want to be in charge of the defining process—as if we were unconnected with that which defines us. This is a highly complicated procedure, but one to which we are so accustomed that we hardly notice it is happening. Rather than allowing ourselves to be continually redefined (and occasionally to be undefined) we demand that we dominate the mutually defining and undefining process that constitutes the flux of reality. We can never have control of this kind, because it would require that each individual be a fixed position within a fixed universe. Shi-nè threatens one's definitions, whatever they are, and reveals, either impishly or demonically, our strong belief in our definitions. Shi-nè displays, either daintily or dreadfully, that we thrive on definitions.

CHAPTER 5

Ocean and Waves

If we can remain in natural uncontrived presence, without sink-
ing into an oblivious drowse, we disinhibit our spontaneous
clarity. Stars appear in the sky, and their brilliance is reflected
in the referenceless ocean of being.

THERE IS NOTHING amiss with anything—but being *in* and *of* the world can be bewildering. A sense of insecurity, vulnerability, incompleteness, wrongness, or lostness can emerge as our reaction to the uncompromising perfection of manifest reality.[1] For this reason, most religions tend to advocate retirement from the world in order to penetrate the nature of bewilderment. There is, however, nothing intrinsically "wrong" with our world. There is nothing wrong with our sense faculties, either. From the perspective of Dzogchen, there is nothing wrong with anything—everything is perfect just as it is. Why, then, is there this sense of wrongness? What is this sense of incompleteness, and where is its origin?

If we look for wrongness in our world, our body, or our perceptual continuum, we can only designate this wrongness according to some sense of "rightness." There has to be some sort of nonproblem or utopian concept of how things should be. Intuiting utopia could be

---

1. Insecurity, vulnerability, incompleteness, wrongness, and lostness relate, respectively, with the five elements: earth, water, fire, air, and space.

construed as an intimation of the enlightened state, but we conceptualize utopia in terms of rejecting the reality of our actual condition,
and thus we merely create another dualistic construction. It is dualistic because we would be projecting a theoretical pure/impure structure
onto reality. This might temporarily distract us from the sense of dissatisfaction we experience, but it would merely reconstruct itself
through its own need for polarization. Ideas that contrast pure and
impure are one mode of perception, but they do not constitute the
only way of understanding reality. If we stepped outside the framework
of polarities such as sin and sanctity, worldly existence and heaven, pain
and release from pain, ignorance and knowledge, confusion and clarity, samsara and nirvana, we could glimpse a vision of our sentient situation in which reality existed outside of polarized parameters.

From the perceptual stance of shi-nè—if we wordlessly observe
our perceptual environment, can we say that it lacks anything? What
should it *have* beyond what it *is*? If we look within ourselves for what
we might lack, can we actually elucidate the nature of what is missing?
What should we have beyond what we are? What is this "incompleteness"? How does this feeling arise if we can discover no basis on
which it could rest? These are peculiar questions, but they may shed
further light on the meaning of the word *Dzogchen*—the uncreated
self-existent completeness.

Being in and of the world can be bewildering, but is there a way in
which we can allow that to open out into a more spacious dimension in which bewilderment might become wonderment?

Profoundly inspired human beings have peered into the question of
existence since the inception of recorded history. Human genius has
propounded philosophies and mystical geometries—but the question,
as far as most people are concerned, remains unanswered. It cannot
be said that there must be an answer. Neither can we say that there is
no answer. All we can say is that we want to *know*, because being in and
of the world is a sticky question. Sometimes the stickiness of the world
is very sweet; it is like honey on the razor's edge. You lick the blade and
"Oh! how very sweet it is!" Then there is the sharpness, and the blood.

Some people would say, "Honey is a wicked and treacherous thing. It is best avoided if you want to avoid being cut." This way of thinking sees the razor's edge of life as undesirable. Some people would say, "Why not find a way of tasting the honey without getting cut?" This is another way of thinking that also sees the razor's edge of life as undesirable. Some people would say, "The razor's edge is all there is—life is nothing but pain; therefore extinction is release." This way of thinking denies the sweetness of the honey. Some people would say, "The honey is all that really matters; if you're cut by the razor's edge then at least you will have tasted the sweetness!" This way of thinking accepts both the honey and the razor's edge but divides the experience. But the honey and the razor's edge are a single experience. If you manifest a human form, you taste the honey on the razor's edge. If you live for the honey and see the razor's edge as an occupational hazard, either your experience of the honey becomes too sickly sweet and makes you vomit or you lacerate yourself on the blade.

What is it to taste the honey on the razor's edge?

Is it to reject the experience of either or both in favor of seeking an answer in nonexistence? Or is it to accept the unified experience as being *what is*, and thus to be liberated from duality?

There are honeyed moments when one feels as if one could live forever. It is true—eternity lives in those moments. But if we try to hang on to eternity, it shrinks rapidly into itself and we find nothing left in ourselves or our environment but artificial divisions. If we continue to lick the razor's edge when the honey has gone, we merely mutilate ourselves—a painful analogy.

Fortunately, or unfortunately, life is not always so extreme. Because it seems so difficult just to *be,* without proof of *being*, we relate to the phenomena of our perception as proofs of existence. We treat our world as a means of substantiating our sentience. We would seem unable to relax into the sensations of enjoying the display. We have to touch and, having touched, we have to grab. Having grabbed, we then have to grasp, defend, possess, strategize, and insulate ourselves with what we have grabbed.[2] It is as if we have had our hands in the honey jar and everything we touch seems unavoidably to adhere. We have sticky fingers.

There is nothing "wrong" with being of the world or in the world, but experientially comprehending the world's perfection is a sticky question. With experientially sticky fingers there is an answer, however: we need to wash our hands in emptiness. Shi-nè has been and will continue to be our preparation for being able to touch with a lessening inevitability of getting stuck.

This idea makes some people anxious. Such people would say, "But the world is so sticky, it is better that you do not touch it in case you get stuck to it." This is a way of thinking in which the world is imagined to be the problem. Others of a more adventurous spirit might be so bold as to say, "Not to touch is dualistic—but we are so sticky that we must continually wash our hands or we will stick to everything." But maybe there is another answer, another approach. We could simply wash our perceptual fingers whenever they appear to be sticky.

At this point, we should look at what these ideas mean in the experience of the Four Naljors. According to Aro Lingma's gTérma of the Four Naljors ngöndro, referentiality is the process of attaching to thoughts in order to provide proofs of existence. Referentiality is an unendingly unfulfilling process. The practice of shi-nè highlights this process and enables us to see what "we" are doing. Reaching out for familiar patterns is what allows thoughts to serve as reference points. But thoughts, ideas, images, feelings, sensations, people, places, and things are not reference points in themselves. They are empty of inherent referential qualities. We merely reduce phenomena to reference points through our fear of ceasing to exist.

The phenomena of the external world are overlaid with the secondary functions that we attribute to them for our pragmatic convenience. A red sky at night betokens fine weather. A red sky in the

2. Grasp, defend, possess, strategize, and insulate relate, respectively, with the five elements: earth, water, fire, air, and space.

morning betokens rain. But these messages are attributed rather than inherent. It is no different with the phenomena of the mental world. With conceptuality, however, it is possible to make this discovery of attribution only through the practice of shi-nè. When one sits, one discovers that the secondary function of thought is to prove that one exists. Without thoughts, one has no reference points. Without thoughts, there is nothing to prove that one is solid, permanent, separate, continuous, and defined. Shi-nè is getting used to that. Shi-nè is simply letting go and letting be.

In everyday life, the continual search for reference points distorts experience in a manner that is largely unsatisfactory. But, although the sensation of unsatisfactoriness irritates or tortures us, we would appear to endure it in order to satisfy our need for self-definition. This is what makes it possible to distract ourselves from *being* by continual attempts to "be"—and this "be" is always manufactured through "do." We *do* "attempting to be solid." We *do* "attempting to be permanent." We *do* "attempting to be separate." We *do* "attempting to be continuous." We *do* "attempting to be defined." This "do style" designs itself on the basis of dualism. The basic misconception is that it is only the form qualities of being that have the capacity to validate existence. Dualistic vision takes existence and nonexistence to be mutually exclusive—and in so doing strays into unending cycles of dissatisfaction and painful confusion. Because we grade what we perceive in terms of its referential value, we are capable of only three responses: attraction, aversion, and indifference. If what is perceived substantiates our personal definitions, attraction arises. If our personal definitions are threatened, aversion manifests. If the phenomena of perception neither substantiate nor threaten our personal definitions, there is indifference. What cannot be manipulated referentially is ignored. We never actually experience anything *as it is*—we only experience according to our need for definitions, and consequently everything is graded as to its suitability as a possible reference point.

There is nothing wrong with thought, even though some categories of meditation instruction would have you accept that there is. According to Dzogchen, thought is a natural function of Mind. Just as the other sense faculties are natural to our physical existence, so is thought. Finding Mind to be a referenceless ocean of space allows the dualistic knot of panic to untie itself. Experiencing this space, we make a brilliant discovery: being referenceless is not death.

If we can remain in natural uncontrived presence without sinking into an oblivious drowse, we disinhibit our spontaneous clarity. Stars appear in the sky, and their brilliance is reflected in the referenceless ocean of being.

Questions and Answers

QUESTION: You were saying that phenomena are empty of inherent referential qualities but that we cramp phenomena into merely being reference points that screen us from our fear of ceasing to exist. Could you give a concrete example?

KHANDRO DÉCHEN: Yes. Ideas such as these probably do take time to digest, so maybe it would be good to look at other kinds of reference points and how they're manipulated. Say you're on a ship and need to navigate—the sun and the stars are useful as reference points. So when we discuss letting go of reference points, we don't intend to suggest the continual loss of one's bearings in the world as a valuable condition. Pragmatic reference points serve a function. We simply need to let go of the *need* to continually reiterate: "I'm located here! This place completely affirms me. I'm real because I know where I am in relation to this map!" We obviously need to function in the relative world, according to relative criteria, but we also need to allow our vision to extend beyond the relative.

NGAKPA CHÖGYAM RINPOCHE: Attaching to people, thoughts, feelings, situations, and objects when they seem to provide existential substantiation is the method by which reference points are established. But reference points always let us down. Reference points always let us down because they, like us, are fleeting facets of a continually changing process.

KD: Everything is transient by nature.

NCR: Some things continue for so long that they seem eternal, but even the sun will eventually die.

KD: The solar system will spiral back into the sun . . .

NCR: . . . and then our pension plans and insurance will be somewhat superfluous.

KD: Yes [*laughs*]. The Himalayas are still rising. Other mountain ranges which once were even higher than the Himalayas are now eroded into hills.

NCR: Certain less grandiose phenomena also outlast us—but we may not be able to remain in their proximity, nor they in ours. Even if cherished possessions remain throughout our lives, the value that we accord them can dwindle into contempt. Sometimes, in reverse, the commonplace becomes valuable. Nothing is stable, but because stability seems so essential, we continually seek proofs from among the momentary manifestations of stability all around us.

Q: Rinpoche, you said that thought and our relationship with it is referentially confused. Could you say more about our relationship with thought?

NCR: Yes, it's our relationship with thought which is in need of a marriage guidance appointment [*laughs*]. It's a referential relationship with thought in which we're simultaneously demanding, petulant, possessive, jealous, and peevish. Thought performs useful functions, but when we relate to our thoughts as reference points they become problematic. It's for this reason that shi-nè is employed as a method that takes us into the condition where thoughts cease to arise. Shi-nè enables us to take a holiday from referentiality.

Q: You said that there's nothing wrong with our world or our sense faculties, from the ultimate perspective, and that there's nothing wrong with anything. . . . How can you say that there's nothing wrong? There's a lot wrong with the world; many people are suffering.

KD: That was not intended to be a political statement. I think we have to make that quite clear. At the relative level, there's certainly a lot wrong with the world. Many people *are* suffering—but where is *your* suffering? This question is being addressed to a spiritual audience, and so we're looking at the world in a different way.

NCR: This doesn't mean that we can't be spiritual people who are also political or social activists. I would imagine that a practitioner would be the best possible social activist. The best person to help other people is someone who doesn't feel like a victim.

KD: A practitioner regards the world as perfect *as* a practice, but that does not mean that he or she regards the suffering of others as perfect.

Q: If attaching to people, thoughts, feelings, and situations because they provide existential substantiation is the method by which reference points are established, and those reference points always let us down, that sounds like the world itself is a letdown in some way.

KD: Not quite [*laughs*]. The world isn't a letdown, unless we attempt to manipulate it. If we try to create reference points out of the presence of the world, then it will always let us down. If the world is left as it is, then it's incapable of letting us down—it supports us endlessly. Actually, reference points are always a letdown, simply because they're nonexistent.

NCR: Glorious, isn't it!

Q: [*laughs*] So . . . if reference points are allowed to be impermanent . . . *then* they can exist?

NCR: Naturally. Whatever you allow to be nonexistent can be existent, and vice versa. That's the deal with duality and nonduality.

KD: If you can allow reference points to be impermanent, then they're no longer the reference points that you actually require them to be.

Q: Could you say a little more about the emptiness of reference points, or give some examples?

KD: Yes. A car is not just a car. A camera is not just a camera. A pair of jeans is not just a pair of jeans. Everything is just a little more or a little less than it seems. If you were to tell someone from a tribal culture who knew nothing of technology about cars, you would probably be quite simple about it. You would give a fairly basic picture. You would talk about transportation, wheels, seats, power source, steering—you would try to give an idea of how a car functioned and how it was of use. But there would be things that you probably wouldn't mention, such as the function of a car as a status symbol, a phallic symbol, a symbol of adulthood, or a hobby.

NCR: There are invariably referential extras attached, which affect the way you relate to everything, and the character of these relationships can often be most inconsistent. When the black paint starts to get rubbed away on your Nikon camera and reveals the brass, you might be pleased because it looks well used—it looks like a professional camera rather than a tourist camera. But if your Mercedes gets its paint scraped in a parking lot, you might not be so pleased. You might not say, "Wonderful! I can see the metalwork through the paint on my Mercedes; now it looks so much more professional!" The older and more faded jeans got, the fonder people were of them—at least when that was the fashion. But people are not so delighted about the dilapidation of their other clothes.

KD: What's acceptable and what's not acceptable often has little to do with the objects themselves. It often has more to do with the role that these objects inadvertently play in making people feel real.

NCR: These things are fairly simple to understand. We can all chuckle about the quirky inconsistencies of status and fashion. But when it comes to the quirkiness and inconsistencies of our own relationship with thought, it's not so easy.

Q: You mentioned that shi-nè is a method that takes you into the condition where thoughts cease to arise. Is this also true of emotions?

KD: Yes.

Q: It seems that emotions are often much stronger reference points than thoughts.

KD: Yes, but for an emotion to be a reference point we have to think about it and relate to it in that way.

NCR: There's a problem here about how we define an emotion and how we define a thought. How do you separate those out in your experience?

Q: I don't really know. I suppose emotions are things that I feel and—

NCR: —and thoughts aren't felt?

Q: Well, yes, I suppose they are . . .

NCR: All you can really say is that there is thought—or rather *namthog*—that which arises in Mind. Namthog can be anything. Some namthogs are emotionally charged, and some seem quite neutral. The stronger the emotional charge, the more we tend to manipulate the namthog in terms of referentiality.

Q: So thoughts and emotions can't really be teased apart?

NCR: It's not worth the attempt—it's simply that whatever arises can either self-liberate or not. We don't have to identify the content of Mind in order to let go of referentiality; we simply have to allow whatever arises to relax into its own condition.

Q: You said that we should let go of saying, "I'm located here; this is a place that affirms me as being real." But isn't that somehow dangerous in terms of developing a healthy sense of yourself in the world?

NCR: Dangerous . . . Well, yes . . . It is dangerous for those at a low level of psychological health. It rather depends on what you need with regard to your psychological development.

KD: I remember, when I was a child, looking up at the stars and feeling friendly about the experience. I knew how to recognize the Great Bear and the Little Bear. I knew how to trace the back leg up from the foot of the Great Bear to find the Pole Star. It was always comforting to recognize my friends in the sky and "know" that in some way something made sense up there. I've never needed to know how to find my bearings by using the stars, so this information has only ever served as a comforting thought, a way of saying to myself, "Ah, yes, there it is—I'm seeing it. I'm a person who knows about that, and now that I've considered that fact, I don't feel quite as lonely or pointless." That was obviously valuable for a child. Children need a sense of concrete reality. But now I'm an adult, so I can look into the question of loneliness and pointlessness. Now I can ask questions about this so-called concrete reality.

PART TWO

PRINCIPAL MEANS OF ENTRY

CHAPTER 6

Flight

These words are a springboard for the discussion of reference-lessness. This springboard is built of ideas designed to undermine ideas. It is intended to enable a leap into the space of referencelessness—a plunge into an understanding of the vastness of what we are.

*I*T COULD COME as a shock to find oneself faced with understandings that may previously have seemed implausible. But to understand explanations that lie beyond the parameters of conventional logic is not an outrageous proposition for anyone who has the enthusiasm to persevere. At this point in our exploration of the first of the Four Naljors, conventional logic will not seem quite the barrier it may have been when we began. From the experience of having worked with the exercises in this book, you will have loosened the tight boundaries of conventional logic a little. You will have the beginnings of a feeling for what lies beyond. But in order to fly into conventionally uncharted regions, your exploration will require practical cooperation in the way of further sitting practice. This practice needs to be interspersed with your reading, and how that evolves will depend upon your own level of understanding.

We would like you to put this book down every time you part company with what is being said in terms of comprehension—and sit. This is the exercise that goes with this chapter. You will need to integrate this practice yourself, with your reading, and according to where you find difficulty in following what is being said. You may or may not need to employ this exercise, but we suggest that you sit at least once a day for half an hour while reading this book in order to have a personal experiential link with what you are reading.[1] This is an experiential book, so unless you already have experience or a strong link with what is being expressed, to read further without practicing will just lead to confusion.

So, as soon as the feeling arises of having parted company with this material, the meaning should be investigated in the light of one's personal sitting experience. There is no point in taking these explanations on trust. It is vital to verify the material through experience. Anything that is accepted for any reason apart from its being consistent with one's firsthand experience will eventually become an obstacle. The method of shin-nè should be employed in order to discover whether these explanations are valid. Explanations can be understood either on the basis of the immediate recognition that originates in practice or from the sparkling-through of one's beginningless enlightened nature. These words are a springboard for the discussion of referencelessness. This springboard is built of ideas designed to undermine ideas. It is intended to enable a leap into the space of referencelessness—a plunge into an understanding of the vastness of what we are.

At this point we would like to discuss two terms that may be helpful in relating to the ways in which different kinds of material can be assimilated. These terms are *conventional logic* and *realized reasoning*. Conventional logic is what is regarded in the world as being acceptable. Realized reasoning is based on experience that lies outside the realm of conventional logic. There is no way in which we can approach the realm of realized reasoning with the battering ram of conventional logic. All we can do is ask how we can arrive at the level of experience from which we will be able to relate to realized

1. This actually applies to the study of any Buddhist method or to hearing oral teachings from Lamas.

reasoning. The answer to this question is made up of methods, the first of which is the practice of shi-nè. Once we have gained some experience of sitting, we will begin to open to the stream of realized reasoning that bases itself on the field of experience into which we have entered. Once open to realized reasoning, we become encouraged to bring everything to the level of experience. The further we take our practice of sitting, the more open we become. Our faculties become less limited by conventional logic. The formerly frustrating barriers between the boundaries of our understanding and the wider horizons of realized reasoning dissolve.

EXERCISE 4

Sit in a posture of comfort and alertness. Find the presence of your awareness only in your exhalation. Allow your inhalation merely to happen. Allow yourself to dissolve your experience into emptiness with each exhalation. If you find that you have drifted from presence, simply return to presence and remain. If thoughts arise, allow them to dissolve into emptiness with each exhalation.

Try this for thirty minutes. See how it goes. If you are used to sitting for longer, sit for as long as you would usually sit. See how it goes.

EXERCISE 4 FOLLOW-UP

This is the final phase of *shi-nè with form*. You have let go of the in-breath, and now you are merely allowing the outflow of your breath to dissolve thoughts or mental imagery into emptiness. You may already have had experiences you could describe as gaps between thoughts, and you may have reacted to them in the various ways described in the previous chapters. Whatever you have experienced, it is now crucial to avoid seeking gaps as a quest. Seeking gaps as a quest is a self-defeating process. The goal of the activity of grasping at gaps cannot be achieved because gaps are only achieved by nongrasping. You may have found that the thought or mental imagery that arose with the in-breath simply dissolved into spaciousness with the out-breath, creating a gap at the end of each exhalation. If you continue to practice in this way, you may find (or you may already have found) that the gap at the end of one out-breath spans several breaths without any mental event manifesting. At this point it becomes possible to enter into the practice of shinnè without form.

You may find that while sitting you get disturbed by subtle tendencies to scatteredness or drowsiness. These manifestations of our energy can be subject to adjustment through a simple exercise involving the head and neck. If you become a little drowsy, you can work with that by jerking your head upward three times. You need to use your discretion here—if you jerk your head up too sharply, you may hurt your neck, and if you don't make a sufficiently decisive movement, the practice will not function particularly well. Likewise, if you feel scattered and unable to settle, jerk your head downward three times.

Once you have repeated this head jerk, you can return to your practice, but if you notice yourself slipping back into drowsiness or scatteredness again, repeat the exercise.

QUESTIONS AND ANSWERS

QUESTION: I'm getting the idea that realized reasoning just happens . . . I think I've had experience of something like that. There is something I can understand there, but at another level I find an aspect of this a bit too abstract and difficult to relate to.

NGAKPA CHÖGYAM RINPOCHE: So I will tell you what it's like to fall out of an aircraft at eighteen thousand feet. I hope that will give you a clearer picture of what we mean by the terms *conventional logic* and *realized reasoning*. If you are a person who enjoys free-fall parachuting, you will have some singular experiences. They'll be ones with which other people cannot easily relate. People might argue with your descriptions unless they have tried free-fall themselves. So . . . let's look at what happens. You fall out of the aircraft. Horror . . .

amazement! You are engaged in an insane act. You were in a perfectly good aircraft, and now you've jumped out of it. . . . But you may as well say, "There I was standing on perfectly good solid ground and then I climbed into this aircraft!"

KHANDRO DÉCHEN: [*laughs*] Or maybe, "There I was, secure in my perfectly good house, and then I went out the front door!" The percentage of the world's population that free-falls is far smaller than the number of those who practice shi-nè.

NCR: The first experience is pretty much what you would expect—you fall like a stone. You fall at the rate of thirty-two feet per second, per second. For the mathematically slow, like myself, this means that you accelerate. It means that you continue to accelerate until you reach what is known as terminal velocity. Terminal velocity is as fast as any unpropelled object can fall on this planet. Terminal velocity is about one hundred and twenty miles an hour, and you reach that speed in about seventeen seconds. That might sound quite terrifying, but something odd happens at terminal velocity that's somehow reassuring—you seem to stop falling. Your stomach catches you up and then it's as if you were being buffeted by the wind.

KD: Free-fallers generally wear what look like oversize clown suits, which enable them to turn and circle on this mysterious column of wind. By falling spread-eagled and adjusting the position of your arms and legs, you're able to circle like an eagle. For a short time you can actually feel like an eagle.

NCR: Yes, you can even observe the curve of the earth and, to some extent, enter the eagle's dimension of perception—a valuable experience for any yogi or yogini. When at last the earth gets too close, you pull the rip cord and the parachute opens. Then the experience changes again. It's still not really like falling, but then, after a while as you look downward, something frankly bizarre happens—it's called "ground rush." It's rather strange. It's a reversal of what people would imagine they would experience. The ground seems as if it's coming up to meet you. So you get into your crouched position and roll when you hit the ground—unless you make your descent with a square canopy, in which case you step out of the sky as if you were stepping off an escalator. Then . . . conventional reality recommences.

KD: Which is why most people want to go straight back up and do it again!

NCR: Now, if you were drawn into discussing your free-fall experience with a dyed-in-the-wool conventional rationalist, you would probably find it quite exasperating. You would say, "How can you argue with me about an experience you've never had?" The rationalist would probably reply that you ought to be able to explain any experience in conventional terms to anyone.

KD: It would be like trying to explain the delight of making love to a lifelong celibate monk or nun.

NCR: [laughs] You would probably question the value of trying to do this and suggest that unless your rationalist were prepared to experience free-fall for himself or herself, he or she would just have to accept what you were saying about it. But the rationalist would be likely to become irritable and antagonistic and say that your description was nonsensical. Such a person might say that it wasn't possible to feel as though you weren't falling when you obviously were falling. He or she might say that you couldn't possibly see the ground coming up at you if you were falling toward it. But in terms of your experience, this argument would seem rather pointless, tiresome, and earthbound. You would say, "Suck it and see, then there might be some value in discussing it." But if people are afraid of flying, they will never find out. They will never know what you're talking about. They might camouflage their fear of flying by saying that if you could prove these things to them by intellectual argument they would be willing to try it—but until then free-falling would just seem like a waste of time with nothing new or strange to experience in it. You would naturally feel rather sad that they weren't open to the possibility of something beyond their conventional frames of reference—but you might not see any value in cramping your experience into the tight box of conventional logic for their dubious benefit.

KD: The tight box of conventional logic can become an avoidance, an evasion, a way around owning up to the fear of flying. You could make all kinds of highly reasonable excuses for not leaping into space. It can actually be something of a relief to cut through the eloquent escapism of erudite excuses and admit to the fear of flying. Somehow, coming to terms with the reluctance to abandon definitions is a positive step—a move toward working with *how you are.*

NCR: To acknowledge the fear of flying is to be open to investigating the nature of fear. From this starting point, fear loosens itself a little. It becomes workable. The idea of sitting becomes a positive challenge rather than an irritating threat. Before boarding an aircraft to make the first jump, the instructor will usually issue a mildly ominous warning, "The only person who's going to come back down to the ground in the aircraft is the pilot. It's a one-way ticket—if you go up, you jump!"

KD: Working with a Lama has something of that quality, as you can see from the allusion to free-falling. If you never board the aircraft, you never make the jump—you're never in the position to jump or to be pushed out into the air. To face the open sky by leaping from an aircraft and to face the open sky of Mind while sitting both require that you face the fear of flying.

Q: You said that because this teaching contains experiential material, reading further without practicing would lead to confusion unless one already had experience or a strong link with the material. What do you mean by a strong link?

KD: An intuitive emotional response. You could say that when there's a certain feeling about the material, it *would* be possible to read without understanding.

Q: And that wouldn't be frustrating?

NCR: Not necessarily—or if it were, it still wouldn't damage the enthusiasm to read on. But this is all highly speculative. I made this comment about strong links because there may be people who have perceptual resonance with this material based on their experience of existence.

CHAPTER 7

Journey into Vastness

One cannot "enact" without affecting everything and, at the same time, being affected by everything. Pattern affects pattern, creating further pattern. Pattern evolves out of chaos and becomes chaos again. Pattern and randomness dance together— ripples in water extend and collide with other extending ripples, a fish leaps to catch an insect, a wild goose takes to the sky, the wind blows, and a child throws a pebble into the lake.

HE SEAS AND oceans of the world are referenceless if one cannot see their boundaries—yet the sun during the day, as well as the moon and stars at night, allow the possibility of navigation for seafarers. The sun, moon, and stars, however, allow this through no intention or design. The ocean of Mind is referenceless—yet the play of Mind's phenomena, arising within its vastness, allows conceptual navigation. This is also achieved through no intention or design beyond the energetic play of that which arises within the nature of Mind. Concepts arise in randomness and pattern—in free flux and direction. The phenomena of Mind create vivid displays that ornament reality as the fundamental nature of compassion.

In our previous discussion, we explored the currents that animate the surface of the ocean of Mind. We explored the need to define "self" as solid, permanent, separate, continuous, and defined. Now we can consider the possibility of gazing at the glittering surface of this ocean of Mind—gazing at the sunlight and starlight glinting. This gazing is an openness that sees with transparence the nature of our relationship with reference points.

Because of our dualized reactions to the sheer naked presence of being,[1] extraordinary games play themselves out as the texture of our life experience. We act as if there were no connection between what we are and where we are—as if there were no connection between "I" and what this "I" has come to describe as the external world. This samsaric speculation propounds a philosophy in which connections are made or broken on the basis of choice—as if we were completely free to insulate ourselves from whatever we regarded as uncomfortable. In terms of the experience of existence, this samsaric philosophy often collides painfully with the natural philosophy of reality. Within this natural, free condition of reality, everything subtly affects and changes everything else—it is not possible to set up a private reality within that without creating a staggering array of complexities.

Any area of interest or involvement (through which one feels drawn by one's perception) is always in the process of continuing modification. There are no static objects. There are no static situations. There are no static beings. There is no static life. The fabric of existence is a fluxing web[2] or magical manifestation web of infinite dimensions. Existence is a fluxing web whose threads are the energy of form and emptiness—of existence and nonexistence. The style or pattern of individual existence sets up tremors in the web of which individual existence is a part. The tensions of the threads alter, and every part of the web is affected. One cannot "enact" without affecting everything and, at the same time, being affected by everything. Pattern affects patterns, creating further pattern. Pattern evolves out of chaos and becomes chaos again. Pattern and randomness dance

---

1. lo-dral jen-pa'i rang-zhal (bLo bral rJen pa'i rang zhal).
2. kun trol (kun khrol). The term *fluxing web* is an awkward English usage but serves to describe the fact that the web is not a permanent pattern but an infinite series of patterns that arise and dissolve into each other. Were kun trol a fixed design, it would be philosophically monist. With regard to Buddhist nonduality, form is necessarily empty, and therefore no fixed pattern can ever be held to have permanent existence.

together—ripples in water extend and collide with other extending ripples, a fish leaps to catch an insect, a wild goose takes to the sky, the wind blows, and a child throws a pebble into the lake.

Nothing in this fluxing web happens in isolation. Isolation is not possible. We cannot isolate "ourselves" from what we conceive of as the external world. We are part of an ocean in which fish and water participate with each other—in which "fish without water" is as untenable as "water without fish." The practice of shi-nè eventually develops into further practices in which horizons of experience open out into greater and more vivid displays of integration. Shi-nè is the gateway to the experiential freedom in which individuation and oceanic experience are not mutually exclusive. When fish and ocean can begin to participate in each other, we realize that many seeming polarities of experience are all aspects of our beginningless enlightenment.

So let us look at oceanic experience. It is usually only infants in arms and certain types of mystics whose experience is oceanic.[3] This is not to suggest that babies are enlightened but to indicate that there are reflections of enlightenment throughout the wide spectrum of human experience. In the case of a baby, oceanic experience is the lack of division experienced between infant and mother—and also between infant and environment in general. From the perspective of inner Vajrayana, every aspect of duality is dynamically linked to a quality of nonduality. So our discussion of oceanic experience is intended to illustrate that this kind of perception is not unknown to human experience outside the field of meditation. The conventional psychological development of the infant leads to individuation. Individuation, however, is usually only achieved at the expense of oceanic experience. There is nothing in early education to encourage the retention of some means of access to oceanic experience.

Society encourages individuation, but the capacity and need for oceanic experience remains. It is part of the spectrum of our human potential. Because it remains, societal influence channels the oceanic

3. Sigmund Freud also used the term *oceanic experience* to describe the way in which young children do not divide themselves from their surroundings.

urge toward family and peer loyalty. Feeling part of something bigger than oneself is important in all civilizations, but the associations formed are not always healthy. Self-centered societal conditioning can distort the oceanic urge into variations of group consciousness such as fascism, racism, elitism, cultism, and religious sectarianism. In conventional human experience, individuation and oceanic experience form an often conflicted counterpoint in the uncomfortable arena of their polarized coexistence. The nature of this conflict also manifests in the world's spiritual persuasions as attachment to distorted reflections of enlightenment that emanate from both individuation and oceanic experience.

Individuated experience gives rise to epistemologies in which creator and created are separate, and in which beings are definite, discrete entities. Oceanic experience gives rise to epistemologies in which creator and created are indivisible and in which the individuality of beings is seen as illusory. From a conventional point of view, it would seem reasonable to assume that fully manifested oceanic experience and completely individuated experience are mutually exclusive. From this point of view it is possible to combine the two only at the expense of both. This is a line of reasoning grounded in dualistic perception, which can only conceive of the divisionlessness of these conventionally polarized experiences as some kind of combination or compromise. Nondual perception, however, does not regress toward infantilism. Neither does it oscillate between polarized perceptions of reality. The experience of enlightenment goes beyond both oceanic and individuated experience and enters into limitlessness, in which such distinctions are meaningless.

This is difficult to grasp. It cannot be grasped intellectually. The very act of grasping distances us from understanding. This situation is much like the free-fall analogy we discussed previously: one is falling yet not falling. Conventional logic has to give up at this point—it can go no further along this road. Conventional logic comes to a halt when it meets a paradox. There is either a spark of understanding that flashes across, or there is incomprehension.

So, we have an idea of dualistic vision in which individuated experience and oceanic experience are polarized. In religious terms, this polarity has given rise to two views of "ultimate reality." In the first view, we "become one" with the universe or we "become one with God." In the second view, we "find eternal life with God," but we find that as separate entities who are divided from him.[4] Religions have created many permutations of these two views, but they all accept either one position or the other. They propose either ultimate loss of individuality or infinite separateness. There is, however, another possibility—but it is possible only if we relinquish the need to establish experiential territory either by making it different from other territories or by making it the same. This possibility is one in which form is emptiness and emptiness is form. In this possibility, patterns continually change. Form emerges from chaos and dissolves back into chaos—chaos and form dance a beginningless dance in which each reflects the other.

Enlightenment is possible at any moment. The intrinsic spaciousness of being is continually reminding us of enlightenment. However, from the disconnected perspective of individuation (divorced from oceanic experience), this reminder is interpreted as a threat to our existence. This could be called *divorced individuation*. Divorced individuation creates the unsteady illusion that fixed definitions are viable. The illusion flickers like an old motion picture. It is possible to catch glimpses of the white screen, but they are conveniently blurred, and the flickering frames melt into each other. There is an unspoken agreement not to suspect that the images seen are not really there. The idea is that we forget that we are watching an intangible that is being projected onto a screen. There is an illusion of solidity, permanence, separation, continuity, and definition, and we relate to that as being real. When watching a film, we have to pretend it is real in order to enjoy it. We have to enter into what is known as "willing suspension of disbelief." With regard to our sense of being, however,

4. The male gender is used because that is the common usage and also because the idea of a creator arises out of the bias toward form (which is male) rather than emptiness (which is female).

we engage in actively determined and continuously prolonged withdrawal of disbelief.

The world of perception teeters precariously between existence and nonexistence. From the perspective of conventionally filtered vision, the phenomena of perception are seductive, provocative, and highly misleading. Substantiality and insubstantiality dance together. One could be looking at a fan dancer: the ostrich plumes of emptiness and phenomena which somehow *are* the voluptuousness of being. Somehow, though, there *is* something else—but we can see what is really there only if we occasionally dispense with the duality of the fans. The naked lady of nonduality is occluded only fleetingly by the flickering feathers of the ostrich-plume fans.[5] Unless this is understood, it is impossible to see what is happening. Unless one realizes that both the lady and her fans are equally naked and equally delightful, one sees nothing but form.[6]

In order to feel solid, permanent, separate, continuous, and defined, one has to attach to facets of the constantly shifting illusion that temporarily display those qualities. One needs to feel solid, permanent, separate, continuous, and defined only because the experience of divorced individuation requires illusion in order to survive. There is a need for struggle in maintaining illusion only because our beginningless enlightenment sparkles through the fabric of duality, continually undermining our manic manipulations.

We are continually poised on the brink of effortlessness, but we continually distract ourselves in order to sustain our sense of divorced indi-

5. The female gender is used because the nondual state is called Kuntuzangmo (kun tu bZang mo, Skt. Samantabhadri—total goodness) in the Aro gTér lineage. Kuntuzangmo is also depicted as the dharmakaya form according to the Tröma Nakmo drüpthab of the Dudjom gTér-sar cycle. Kuntuzangmo is the female equivalent of Kuntuzangpo (kun tu bZang po, Skt. Samantabhadra—total goodness), who is more generally used in the Nyingma tradition. Künzang yab-yum (Kuntuzangmo and Kuntuzangpo in sexual union) is an anthropomorphic representation of the nondual state. The term *goodness* should not be understood as being the opposite of "badness." The goodness of Kuntuzangmo is one of absolute inclusiveness, wholeness, or even wholesomeness.

6. Nakedness (chèr-bu, gCer bu) and delight (kuntu ga, kun tu dGa') equate with emptiness and form.

viduation. These delirious, distressing, and dreary deviations from effortlessness are mechanisms we employ in order to maintain the illusion of duality. These mechanisms are constantly under threat of disillusionment. Disillusionment is the continuous nondual intimidation offered by the nature of reality itself, and from the experience of this intimidation there arises a specific kind of dualistic self-protective activity. This activity can be described as that of generating commitment to fleeting apparitions of stability. This is the character of duality.

Nonduality, on the other hand, is completely relaxed in the flow of *whatever is*. It could be said that if all phenomena had a duration of minutes, and everything changed simultaneously everywhere, a state of distraction might not be able to maintain itself. Nothing that comes into existence has the qualities of solidity, permanence, separateness, continuity, or definition. These qualities can never be found as fixed features of anything, yet everything shares these qualities temporarily. Therefore, it becomes possible to generate illusory versions of reality. But these versions of reality are simply further fan dances, where the ostrich plumes are either substantiality and insubstantiality, permanence and impermanence, separateness and indivisibility, continuity and discontinuity, or definition and indefinability. These fan dances are neither samsara nor nirvana. They are ornaments of the sheer naked presence of being.

EXERCISE 5

Sit in a posture of comfort and alertness. Find the presence of your awareness to be without focus. If you drift from presence of awareness, return to presence of awareness without comment or judgment. If mental events manifest, remain uninvolved. Let go and let be. Continue to let go and let be. Relax completely. Try this for between forty minutes and an hour, depending on how long you are able to sit. If you are currently sitting for less than an hour, gradually build up until you can sit for an hour. If you are used to sitting for longer, then sit for however long you find comfortable. See how it goes.

EXERCISE 5   FOLLOW-UP

This is the conclusion of the practice of shi-nè, but not the conclusion of practice. Shi-nè takes us to the experience of time without content—mind without mental events. The purpose of shi-nè is to facilitate an experience of Mind in which one discovers referencelessness. This is the realization of emptiness and the knowledge that thoughts or mental events are not in themselves the fabric of Mind. The nature of Mind is sheer brilliant emptiness. The instruction/direction at this stage of practice is to remain in this empty state and to enter into what is known as stabilized shi-nè.

Stabilized shi-nè is a condition of Mind in which mental events no longer arise for substantial periods within one's sitting sessions. Having reached the stage at which one is able to let go and let be, able simply to continue, one will have momentarily exhausted the neurotic desire to generate thoughts in order to establish reference points.

As soon as shi-nè is stabilized, one faces a new challenge. At this point, a potential problem can manifest and will need to be resolved if practice is to continue to develop. This problem is termed "sleepy shi-nè." It is a state in which mental events are absent, but in which presence of awareness is also absent. It is at this point that shi-nè needs to be dissolved by entering into lha-tong. Lha-tong means "further vision" and represents the way beyond emptiness—the real beginning of the journey into vastness.

CHAPTER 8

Beyond Emptiness

*When fabulous glistening fish leap into existence from noth-
ingness, exploding the brilliant mirror surface of the lake, there
are immediately three vital considerations: the still lake, the
leaping fish, and the awareness that is present in both.*

BEYOND THE EXPERIENCE of emptiness[1] is the experience
of how energy manifests as the endless display of Mind. It
is often imagined that the final goal of practice is to attain a condition of mind in which thought has been entirely abandoned. It is
not surprising that this idea exists, because many forms of meditation instruction deal with the stabilization of shi-nè. It is not unusual that in such teachings little emphasis is placed on what lies
beyond emptiness.

There is nothing false about explanations that posit emptiness as
the fruit, and those who explain in this way are perfectly correct
according to the view of the specific practices they describe.[2] According to many teachings within the Sutras, emptiness *is* the goal—but
Dzogchen requires subtlety and precision with regard to how emptiness is defined as being *an aspect of the goal.* This is not particularly

---

1. mi-thogpa, the state of no content of mind, no mental manifestations, no namthogs.
2. Teachings are given according to specific *yanas,* or vehicles, and these teachings differ in their emphasis according to the principle of the particular path.

controversial, because the *Heart Sutra* states quite succinctly that form is emptiness and emptiness is form.[3]

The aspect of Sutra that equates with form is compassionate activity. Form is never seen as separable from emptiness within the enlightened state. Therefore, emptiness must ultimately be considered in terms of dualistic and nondual experience. If emptiness and form are nondual, then the experience of emptiness must relate with the unimpeded arising and dissolving of form. From this perspective, emptiness without relation to form could simply be the most rarefied manifestation of dualism. But let us examine the matter in closer detail. Emptiness is the fruit of the practice of shi-nè. The end result of this practice is the absence of namthog—arising thought.[4] But although the absence of namthog is the end result of shi-nè, it is not the end of practice and it is not realization. There are further stages of practice, and these deal with the energies that continually manifest as the natural function of emptiness. These also deal with the reintegration of energy with the presence of awareness.

The discovery of emptiness is a stage in the process of realizing our beginningless enlightenment. But if we get too stuck on the idea of resting in the space of Mind without content, it becomes a spiritual cul-de-sac. Mind without thought is as unnatural a condition as Mind crowded with thought. So why have we come all this way merely to experience another limited state of being? In order to answer this question, we need to explore ourselves a little further and ask ourselves what we take Mind to be.

Without meditative experience, even examination or investigation of the conceptual mind would be rather limited. If we looked at the nature of Mind (in the usual way we look at things) in order to find out what it is, all we would find would be mental events. We would be confronted with thoughts: the thoughts under obser-

3. nying mDo (sNying mDo), Heart Sutra. Chomden Déma Shérab Kyi Pharoltu Jinpa'i Nyingpo (bCom lDan 'das ma shes rab kyi pha rol tu phyin pa'i sNying po), the Bhagavati Prajñaparamita Hridaya Sutra.
4. *Namthog* (rNam rTog) means "that which arises in Mind." Namthogs can be anything, not simply thoughts but also patterns, colors, textures, and feelings.

vation and the thoughts that constituted the method of observation. If this were the only way we could observe Mind, all we could ever uncover would be an endless series of thoughts. This self-limiting activity would never uncover the nature of Mind—it would just ensnare us in an intellectual kaleidoscope that never stopped revolving. Unfortunately, that would be the end of our quest whether we realized it or not. We would imagine that Mind *was* thought, and that would be the end of our exploration. If we examined the nature of Mind's phenomena using thought as our tool, we would be limited by the character of the thought structures at our disposal. We would be examining thought with thought—and that would become progressively more ludicrous. The thoughts with which we examined thought would have to be examined, and what would examine those thoughts apart from more thoughts, which would also need to be examined? Thought cannot ultimately examine itself—it is a closed system. Thought can no more examine itself than a knife can cut itself or an eye see itself. The only way that an eye can see itself is in a mirror—and the nature of that mirror (as far as thought goes) is the natural reflective capacity of Mind, which is beyond thought.

This natural reflective capacity of Mind is discovered through the various forms of practice outlined in this book. These practices take us beyond the limitations of intellectual speculation. To investigate the nature of thought, we need to use some capacity other than thought. In order to discover what other methods we have for investigating the nature of thought, we need to detach ourselves from our obsessive relationship with thought. So, shi-nè (the practice of remaining uninvolved with thought) is where we start. In your practice of shi-nè, you will have spent time "letting go and letting be"—and maybe by now you have been able to witness the fact that Mind is not thought alone. When we first look at Mind (without the practice of thought-free observation), all we are able to see is a flat screen of thought. We see Mind as a patchwork or a pastiche of interlocking, overlapping thoughts. It is as if we were looking at the surface of a lake ruffled by the wind or the sky churning with dark clouds. From these impressions, no one would have any idea that the surface of the lake could be like a mirror perfectly reflecting the sky, or that behind the clouds lay the infinity where the sun shone or the moon and stars glittered within the vastness of space. If we rigged up some sort of wind generator in order to examine the lake, we would merely create more disturbance, and all we would learn would be that waves can become more pronounced. We would gain no idea of the natural reflective capacity of the lake. If we set up a gigantic cauldron that issued up yet more water vapor into an already overcast sky, we would not be likely to get any insight into the nature of the sky with regard to its capacity to manifest clouds.

But when involvement with thought is retracted, the turbulence diminishes. The cloud cover becomes patchy, the wind dies down, and we begin to see reflections on the surface of the lake. Occasional gusts may ruffle the surface again, but now we know that water is not always in motion—sometimes it is still. When thoughts cease to be generated as an obsessive process, the clouds begin to part. Odd shafts of sunlight strike through. The occasional trace of blue is seen. As soon as the realization dawns that the flat screen of thought is a construction, we are able to facilitate the process of discovering emptiness.[5]

Once we have discovered emptiness and found that we can exist without reference points, we need to discover our natural relationship with the energy that is the spontaneous manifestation of emptiness. The free nature of Mind is neither a flat screen of thought nor an emptiness in which nothing happens. Both are partial conditions. But once we have learned that we can let go of thought, our relationship with thought can open up into something more fluid, frictionless, and nonadhesive. It may come as a surprise that thought is not antithetical to the enlightened state. Often when meditation is spoken of, the emphasis is on the abolition of thought. Because of this, a lot of people come to the conclusion that thought itself is the enemy. But thought is a natural function of Mind. Where noth-

5. The flat screen of thought is what is initially seen when shi-nè is practiced.

ing arises from emptiness, there is no energy and, consequently, no clarity.[6]

The reason for continuing to practice in order to arrive at a state without thought is that it provides the space to unlearn our neurotic relationship with thought. If we return to the idea that meditation *isn't*; getting used to *is*, we can see that the process, or space of unlearning, is *getting used to* the referenceless quality of being. Letting go of neurotic involvement with thought can be looked at in a similar way to letting go of a drinking problem. If one wants to stop being an alcoholic, one might have to stop drinking for some time. But if one never feels safe to drink again without the fear of returning to alcoholism, then one is still an alcoholic—an abstemious alcoholic. The time spent resisting the inclination to get drunk and the number of days undergone without a sense of deprivation are a significant learning process. Time is being deployed, in this case, to prove that alcohol is not needed in order to live. Once one has the certainty that drunkenness is no longer a refuge, one can drink and see what happens.[7] If the immediate impulse is to drink compulsively, one knows that one is still an alcoholic. But if one or two glasses suffice, one is free to have a glass of wine over a meal with a friend or whenever it is appropriate. But still, one would have to watch oneself carefully. Even a glass a day anticipated a little too eagerly might indicate a degree of dependence, and one might have to abstain again for periods of time.

So it is with everything, with thought, and with all phenomena. When we can enter into a condition without thought and remain present and awake in that experience for extended periods of time, we know that our relationship with thought has undergone a radical change. This is stabilized shi-nè, and once we have established ourselves in this practice, we can dissolve shi-nè and enter into the practice of lha-tong.

6. The natural movement of namthogs within the space of Mind is known in the Dzogchen tradition as *sel* (gSal), clarity.
7. This description of alcoholism, while an accurate analogy for the meditative process, is not presented as recommended behavior for anyone who is or has been an alcoholic.

The dissolution of shi-nè can seem to be the destruction of everything we have sat so long to accomplish—but it is a vital part of the process if we are interested in continuing the journey into vastness. Unless shi-nè is dissolved, there is a chance of becoming addicted to absence. A practitioner who simply remained with absence of thought could become an absence addict rather than a thought addict. It is difficult to remain for long in stabilized shi-nè without drifting into sleepy shi-nè. It is very relaxing to dwell in the condition of sleepy shi-nè, and, from the initial standpoint of never having practiced, it could even seem like an accomplishment. The danger of sleepy shi-nè is that (without this warning) one might well take this state to be the end result of practice, and that would be a depressing conclusion. It is a shame to become fixated on any idea. One should always attempt to remain open to anything that contradicts one's most cherished beliefs.

In order to dissolve shi-nè, we have to allow namthogs to reemerge, but not by reengaging in the neurotic process of generating reference points. When we dissolve shi-nè and allow the natural energy of Mind to reemerge from emptiness, we are not creating anything, we are simply *allowing*. As soon as energy starts to reemerge, all that can be done is to allow the energy freedom to manifest and to find the presence of awareness both in its emergence from emptiness and in its dissolution into emptiness. This type of experience is often likened to the leaping of fish from the still surface of a lake.

When fabulous glistening fish leap into existence from nothingness, exploding the brilliant mirror surface of the lake, there are immediately three vital considerations: the still lake, the leaping fish, and the awareness that is present in both. The still lake is emptiness or the absence of namthogs. There is nothing there but presence. This is the discovery of shi-nè. The leaping fish, or the arising namthogs (texture/color/pattern/thought/sensation), move without referential coordinates. This is the discovery of lha-tong.

Initially, the practice of dissolving shi-nè and wordlessly observing the jumping fish from the still lake is known as lha-tong. Lha-tong means "further vision." It is an extraordinarily vivid experience. It is vivid because, for the first time, thought is no longer experienced as two-dimensional. Mind is no longer a flat screen composed of over-lapping, interlocking sequences of thought. Namthogs arise in a spatial context. Lha-tong allows the experience of color, texture, and tone. With the practice of lha-tong, we find the presence of awareness in the movement of the energy that arises from the empty state. Within this spaciousness we can ultimately find moments of instant presence, or nondual recognition of being.[8] In this way, the movement of arising and dissolving namthogs becomes the nature of the path.

One method of allowing fish to jump is to open the eyes completely. But having opened your eyes, you may well lose yourself through grasping on to thoughts again. At this point, it is very likely that you could become rather frustrated. To open the eyes and find the presence of awareness in whatever arises is simple, but not necessarily easy. This movement of namthogs—this jumping of the fish from the clear lake of stabilized shi-nè—is called gYo-wa.[9] gYo-wa means "movement," and it is in this movement that we have to find the presence of our awareness—rather than losing presence through attachment to the conceptual content of the moving namthogs. We make no comment on the namthogs. We make no judgments as to whether these are beautiful or grotesque fish that are jumping. We simply find the presence of awareness in their movement. We allow ourselves to become identified with that which moves.

Having reached this point, we need to discuss the nature of practice again. While we engage in the practice of lha-tong, problems of lack of presence or distraction can be mediated. This is possible through specific methods that relate directly with the functioning of energy at the levels of mind, voice, and body. The three exercises on the following pages work with energetic imbalances and will prove helpful at this stage of practice.

We have outlined the primary practice according to the system of shi-nè and lha-tong. Now it is important to look at some

8. "Instant presence" is one of a number of ways in which *rigpa* can be translated. There is also nondual awareness, presence of awareness, and nondual presence.
9. gYo ba.

complementary methods. These auxiliary practices belong to the categories of mind, voice, and body and relate to the three spheres of being: *chö-ku, long-ku,* and *trül-ku.* Chö-ku is the sphere of unconditioned potentiality—the dimension of emptiness. Long-ku is the sphere of intangible appearance—the dimension of energy (the infinite display of light and sound). Trül-ku is the sphere of realized manifestation—the dimension of physicality.[10] Whatever problem of distractedness arises, one begins at the level of mind. If that proves ineffective, one moves to the level of voice. If that is fruitless, one moves to the level of body. The three exercises that follow are methods of these three levels and should be practiced in succession as shown.

EXERCISE 6

Sit in a posture of comfort and alertness. Close your eyes and visualize the Tibetan letter *A* as shown (figure 1). The letter *A* is white, luminous, and composed of light. It appears in space in front of you. Its position should be governed by raising your arm in front of you 45 degrees to the horizontal and visualizing the *A* at the distance of your clenched fist. The *A* should normally be about the same size as your fist, but allow it to be whatever size feels most comfortable or whatever size it spontaneously takes.

Although your eyes are closed, look upward slightly as if you were focusing on the point where your fist would be. Hold your arm in front of you for a while until the visualization becomes reasonably stable. Lower your arm and continue to find the presence of your awareness in the appearance of the *A*.

Try this for three five-minute intervals within your sitting sessions. If you are used to visualization, try this for ten-minute intervals during whatever length of sitting feels comfortable. At the end of these intervals, allow the *A* to dissolve and continue to find the presence of your awareness in whatever arises.

10. A realized human being (tulku), or a realized being in other locations or dimensions.

FIGURE 1: *A*

EXERCISE 6   FOLLOW-UP

As this may well have been your first experience of visualization, you may have encountered some difficulties that interfered with the efficacy of this practice. You may have found working with a letter from another alphabet an alienating experience. If you found the shape of the *A* strange or complex, it would be a good idea to copy the *A* as illustrated here and look at it intently before beginning the exercise. The act of tracing the shape will help you remember it, especially if you draw it several times. You could paint it in white on a large, dark-blue piece of cardboard, which could be placed at eye level where you usually sit. The more often you engage in this practice, the more familiar you will become with the shape of the *A*, until you will be able to visualize it easily. You may find that the *A* moves around a lot at first. If it does, do not worry about it—just leave it to settle down on its own. Try to avoid fixing your attention too sharply for too long. Focus sharply at first, but then relax your focus. If the *A* is not particularly vivid, do not dwell on disappointment—just allow it to be a vague presence. There is no need to expect competence in visualization immediately. Work with this practice for at least a week before continuing to the voice method of exercise 7.

EXERCISE 7

Sit in a posture of comfort and alertness. Leave your eyes open. Take several deep breaths. Having filled your lungs, sing the sound of *A* and extend that sound to the limit of your breath. (The sound is "ah.") Sing the *A* at a good, deep pitch, but not so deep that your voice weakens and breaks up. Find your most comfortable pitch and settle into it. Allow the *A* to attenuate gradually and disappear into silence. Repeat the *A* with each out-breath. Allow your sense of being to be flooded by the sound of the *A*. Find the presence of your awareness in the dimension of the sound. Whenever distracted, return to the presence of awareness in the dimension of the sound.

Try this for five-minute intervals within whatever length sitting session you find comfortable. Enter into the practice of singing the *A* whenever you become distracted.

EXERCISE 7 FOLLOW-UP

The syllable *A* is known as the natural sound of the primordial state. Singing the *A* relaxes your vocal energy—the resonance permeates your being and diffuses the tensions created through attempts to establish concrete definitions of what you are. Singing *A* enables you to enter into a more open recognition of the spaciousness of being. *A* is known in the Tibetan tradition to be a neutral sound, and as such it allows your vocal energy to enter into its natural resonance without any undue effort. The sensation of singing *A* and letting the sound attenuate into silence can be rather like a deep sigh—it facilitates the dissolution of patterned perception, leaving you feeling clear and relaxed. Because the energy of the voice is more tangible than the apparition of the visualized *A*, you can use the *A* sound when visualization seems too difficult or fruitless in terms of allowing you to return to presence of awareness. Work on this practice for at least a week before continuing to the body method of exercise 8.

EXERCISE 8

This exercise *can* have fatal consequences. Do *not* attempt this exercise under *any* circumstances if you have a heart condition or high blood pressure. Do *not* attempt this exercise if you are pregnant or menstruating. If you are in *any* doubt whatsoever about your physical condition, *please do not attempt this exercise.* This is a serious warning.

Squat down on tiptoe. The balls of your feet should be touching. Your heels should be touching. Balance yourself by touching the ground in front of you with your fingertips.

When you feel balanced, place your palms on your knees. Straighten your arms. Push your knees downward a little. Spread your knees apart and straighten your back. Lean back a little rather than fail to find your back in a vertical position.

When you feel balanced, raise your hands above your head. Place the palms of your hands firmly together about an inch above your head (figure 2). Ensure that your fingers are pointing directly upward. Simultaneously attempt to push your hands up and your elbows back without separating your hands or allowing your hands to rise further above your head. These two movements should be matched in effort so that they counteract each other. If you put equal effort into both movements, your hands and arms will remain in the same position. Increase the effort until your hands and arms begin to shudder. Make sure that your fingers are still pointing upward and not leaning either forward or backward.

Now raise yourself until your legs form the same angle as your arms (figure 3). Remain in that position until you collapse. This should not take longer than a minute, unless you are an experienced hatha yogi or yogini.

FIGURE 2: *Vajra Posture 1*

Fall back onto a cushion and sit, still stressing your arms. Remain in that posture until you can no longer hold it. This should not take long.

Fall back into the corpse posture (flat on the floor with your arms at your sides). Remain in that posture until your breathing and heart rate have returned to normal.

While lying down, just let go and let be. While at any stage of the practice, just let go and let be. When you sit up again, continue in your sitting practice. This practice will last no more than

FIGURE 3: *Vajra Posture 2*

a minute or two (for most people) as far as holding the stressed posture. The relaxed posture will vary according to your fitness but should not last beyond three or four minutes. Try to avoid lying down for too long, or you may well lose the sense of alertness and freshness that comes from this practice. Repeat this practice as many times as feels comfortable.

EXERCISE 8   FOLLOW-UP

This practice of body is called the vajra posture, or thunderbolt posture.[11] The shape of the posture mirrors the shape of the vajra. It symbolizes the indestructibility of our primordial state of awareness. The three spheres of being are often called the three vajras, illustrating that the integrated condition of these three spheres of being is beyond conditioning.

The principle of this practice is *nalma*, or exhaustion.[12] Through a highly specific method of exhaustion we are able to exhaust our neurotic involvement with thought as the definition of being. In the state of nalma it is difficult to conceptualize. Through nalma it can become easier to enter into a condition in which we can drop our frames of reference. In a state of nalma we find ourselves far less interested in generating thought merely to identify and fix reference points. But there is a problem with exhausting ourselves—it tends to cause tiredness. The longer it takes to become exhausted, the longer it takes to recover from that exhaustion. The longer it takes to recover, the sleepier we become in the process of recovery.

Vajra posture is the answer to this problem, inasmuch as it enables us to reach the state of nalma extraordinarily quickly. Because of the speed with which nalma is reached, recovery from the symptoms of exhaustion is also very quick. Because of this, we are left feeling energized, clear, and refreshed. The high-speed quality of this practice is important. If it takes too long to reach the state of nalma, we need to improve the posture so that it becomes more painful.

The idea of causing ourselves pain is not particularly appealing, but the point of arriving at the most painful possible position is that as soon as we have found it, we collapse. This should occur within seconds rather than minutes, as this practice should not cause pain beyond the duration of the exercise. Neither should it

---

11. It takes its name from the dorje (rDo rJe), literally, "lord stone," which accompanies the bell (drilbu, dril bu) in Tantric rites.

12. *Nalma* (rNal ma) means "natural state."

cause physical damage. Appropriate pain, in this context, is the pain that athletes experience. Athletic pain can make us realize that we are actually alive in a physical body. Practice is not oriented toward forgetting that we have a physical manifestation as well as a body of energy and spaciousness. This practice involves our awareness and our honesty with ourselves. If we do not stress the arms sufficiently, or work to find the exact position that causes the legs the most stress, we hold the posture for too long. The principle is to spend as little time as possible in the posture, so that our recovery rate is proportionately fast.

Depending on who you are and what you are like, you will find different problems with the posture. If you are stiff and unused to using your body, you may have to squat down with your feet slightly apart, and not in such a high kind of tiptoe. If you are just unfit, you may have no problem at all as long as you are fairly supple and have a sense of balance. If you do not have a developed sense of balance, this posture will help you center yourself and discover a greater sense of emotional/psychological equilibrium as well. Physical balance and emotional balance are interrelated, so it is helpful to work at this practice every day, if possible. Some people may be quite fit and have a great deal of stamina but little sense of balance. How you are will give you something different with which to work.

The vajra posture is part of the *trül'khor naljor*[13] system. This has some superficial similarities to hatha yoga, but it is different in a number of essential respects—especially with regard to the vajra posture as described here. Attainment of the perfect posture is not the principle here—nalma is. Reaching the state of nalma in the quickest possible time is what matters most with the vajra posture. So, if you have some experience of hatha yoga, please do not approach this exercise with the same attitude—especially if you are

---

13. 'khrul 'khor rNal 'byor, Skt. yantra yoga. Usually found within the Anuyoga and Anuttarayoga classes of Tantra. However, the trül'khor method of vajra posture described here is taken from a system related to Dzogchen Sem-dé.

FIGURE 4: *Vajra*

accustomed to the kind of hatha yoga in which you are advised to use force and willpower beyond a reasonable limit. The principle is nalma, so it is important to discover the exact point where the angle of your legs will lead to almost instant collapse. If you are used to practicing hatha yoga, you may be superbly supple, and if this is the case, you will need to make the posture as exact as you can. The more supple you are, the more you will have to make this posture *work*—and for this you will have to use your awareness.

The posture can be made more acute by perfecting the symmetry. This can be achieved by placing the soles of your feet flat together in the same way as you press your hands together, and by pushing your knees further apart. You will notice the similarity to the drawing of the vajra (figure 4). So, whatever your physical capacity or incapacity, it is vital to tailor this posture to work in the best possible way for you.

If you are inspired by the possibility of visualization, there is an internal aspect to this practice that involves visualizing yourself as a dark-blue vajra (figure 4) surrounded by sky-blue flames. Within the sphere at the center of the vajra is the sky-blue syllable *Hung* (figure 5). As you breathe in, the *Hung* contracts to the size of one little fingernail. As you breathe out, the *Hung* expands until it becomes larger than the vajra of your body.

This will intensify the power of the practice, but if you find this too complicated, simply find the presence of your awareness in the sensation of the posture. As with all such instructions on visualization, one should seek transmission in order for the method to function authentically.

QUESTIONS AND ANSWERS

QUESTION: Khandro Déchen, you were saying that through nalma it can become easier to enter into a condition where you can drop your frames of reference, and that in the state of nalma you find yourself less interested in generating thoughts. Could you elaborate on that?

KHANDRO DÉCHEN: If you've ever run for a bus—I'm thinking of a London bus without a door but with a pole you can grab hold of to pull yourself on board—if you've just brought yourself to the verge of collapse after a heart-bursting sprint through the traffic fumes, you'll have some idea of what we mean when we say exhaustion inhibits conceptuality. Imagine collapsing into the nearest vacant seat with eyes bulging and heart pounding [*laughs*]. Then at this point the bus conductor asks you where you're going. Maybe at that precise

FIGURE 5: *Hung*

moment you hardly know where you are, let alone where you came from or where you could be going.

Q: Right . . . I remember something similar. So could I use that too?

KD: Why not? Apart from the fact that there would be tiredness accompanying the exhaustion, which would tend to make you sleepy.

Q: I have heard that sleepy shi-nè is dangerous—that it's a very serious error to fall into with formless practice.

NGAKPA CHÖGYAM RINPOCHE: Yes, that is said . . . But there's nothing actually so terrible about sleepy shi-nè for the average person.

KD: It could even be a way to wind down a little after a hard day at work. But getting stuck in that condition doesn't actually help you work with your life to any great extent. We have met a number of people who've taken meditation to this point, and sometimes they've been irritated by hearing us speak of practices beyond emptiness. In fact, on hearing us say that stabilized shi-nè wasn't the ultimate practice, one person decided he had had enough and left! For him maybe it was a serious error of some kind.

Q: I once heard a Buddhist teacher say, "There is no thought in the mind of a Buddha." How does that relate to the teaching of Dzogchen? There seems to be some contradiction here.

KD: It's not really possible to comment on that without knowing the whole context of what was said. However . . . there is no attachment to thought in the Mind of a Buddha. There is also no conceptual limitation in the Mind of a Buddha.

NCR: The idea that Mind without content is the conclusion of the path is almost like saying enlightenment is becoming a statue of a Buddha. There seems to be the notion among many people that the longer you sit in the thought-free state, the more enlightened you'll become.

KD: But to the question "What process is at work in this empty state that leads toward complete enlightenment?" the answer is usually that such things are ineffable and cannot be expressed in words. It is true that words are limited and that enlightened experience is beyond concept—but if we're speaking of *process*, it can always be described by someone who has experienced that process. Unless your practice continues into the process of integration, you stultify. We need to open ourselves to flowing with whatever arises within this empty state we have discovered. Unless we are prepared to engage in that practice, we will not evolve into full recognition of what we really are. And without this recognition, the general character of our life experience will not change much. We will continue to experience unsatisfactoriness, frustration, and turmoil.

Q: Rinpoche, I've heard some people being critical of public teaching of vajra posture, because it's supposed to be very secret and only taught to people in three-year retreat. It seems confusing when different teachers present contradictory teachings and methods. Why do some people regard vajra posture as secret and others speak about it openly? I hope you don't find this question impolite, because I know that several Tibetan Lamas teach vajra posture . . . but there seems to be some problem here that I'm not understanding.

NCR: Maybe I could start by asking some general questions about this subject. Why is anything secret?

Q: I presume because certain things might be dangerous?

NCR: Yes. That's a good reason. In Britain, certain glues are kept "secret" because some young people have found they can intoxicate themselves by inhaling the fumes. These glues are secret with regard to the fact that they're locked up. You have to ask for them, and you have to be over a certain age to buy them. This also applies to alcohol and cigarettes. There are many other reasons for secrecy, obviously. A birthday present is usually kept secret until one's birthday—and the reason is that it's supposed to be a surprise. One's sexual relationship is kept secret or hidden, because of the need to protect its intimacy or specialness.

KD: But then you go to certain cities and you can see advertisements offering the spectacle of "live sex acts on stage." Obviously, people have different ideas of what is secret. These ideas change according to time, place, and culture. A respectably dressed woman on holiday at the seaside might look completely indecent to a member of a strict Islamic society. It would seem that people have highly divergent ideas about what is to be kept secret and what is open, and many conflicting reasons for secrecy and openness can exist, not only between different cultures but within the same culture. So that's one answer to your question—according to social anthropology.

NCR: You will find that there is always a reason for secrecy, and that reason will be enshrined in some kind of system. In Buddhism, the reasons for secrecy, and the categories of teachings that are held to be secret, depend on the vehicle. The view that trül'khor naljor is secret comes from the Anuttarayoga Tantras.[14] From that perspective, it is important to practice *kyé-rim* before *dzog-rim*[15]—and obviously if a certain teacher is teaching from that perspective, he or she will emphasize the importance of keeping higher teachings concealed until they can be practiced.

KD: It is not useful to know about practices if you can't put them into practice fairly immediately.

Q: Why is that?

KD: Well, simply put, you open the packet quite soon before you eat the contents. You don't open the bottle and leave it standing for a couple of years before you drink it. This applies to teachings as much as it does to food and wine.

NCR: The teachings become stale with regard to the transmission if they're simply collected as information with no immediate application. So let us now look at the vajra posture. The vajra posture as we have taught it has its origin in Dzogchen Sem-dé rather than in the Anuttarayoga Tantras, and so it exists within a different framework,

14. The Anuttarayoga Tantras belong mainly to the Sarma or New Translation schools of Tibetan Buddhism—Sakya, Kagyüd, and Gélug. They are divided into the Father, Mother, and Nondual categories in the Sakya and Kagyüd schools, and into the Father and Mother categories in the Gélug school.
15. Kyé-rim (bsKyed rim) and dzog-rim (rDzogs rim) are the development and completion phases of Tantra. Kyé-rim concerns the visualization of awareness-beings, and dzog-rim concerns the spatial channels, spatial winds, and spatial-elemental essences.

one in which secrecy is not required. You will find that the visualization taught here is different from the visualization given with other systems of trül'khor naljor. I know this because I have received several lineage teachings on trül'khor naljor and so I am aware of the differences. You will also find that the instructions on the posture are also different. In the Aro gTér Sem-dé trül'khor, the emphasis is more on developing the experience of nalma.

Q: The principle of this practice is exhaustion?

KD: Yes, but in the sense of nalma, the exhaustion of concept, through a highly specific method that links physical exhaustion with the exhaustion of clinging to concept. That kind of exhaustion practice is called nalma. It's not the same as merely exhausting yourself physically. With nalma, you exhaust your neurotic involvement with thought as the definition of being.

Q: You said that the vajra posture symbolizes the indestructibility of our primordial state and illustrates the integrated condition. Could you explain what *integration* means in this context?

NCR: The word *integration* is used a lot in the Dzogchen teachings.[16] It comes into every aspect of practice. Integration simply means that nothing is separate from the nondual state. The three spheres are described as indestructible because they have never been separate from the nondual condition. Integration means moving beyond the stage of practice where ordinary life and practice exist as separate experiences.

KD: The vajra posture is a physical symbol of that—both as a means of transmission and as a method of realizing the nature of that transmission.

16. nyam-nyid ngag (mNyam nyid ngag), integration.

PART THREE

INTERFACE WITH TOTALITY

CHAPTER 9

The Vivid Portal

It is actually not possible to practice nyi'mèd—at a certain stage of practice, nyi'mèd simply happens. It happens when we find ourselves moving without design between the states of shi-nè and lha-tong. This natural movement simply presents itself, of itself—as soon as one finds the presence of awareness in the dimensions of nè-pa and gYo-wa.

SIMULTANEOUS AWARENESS[1] OF the clear lake and the leaping fish is our first glimpse of nondual experience. This is the discovery of nyi'mèd and the vivid portal of Dzogchen.

In our previous discussions of shi-nè and lha-tong, we described the manner in which namthogs arise: the fish leaping into existence from emptiness and exploding the surface of the lake. At this point there are immediately three vital considerations: the still lake, the leaping fish, and the awareness that is present in both.

Before we discuss the awareness that is simultaneously present in the still lake and the leaping fish, we should understand something of the context in which these considerations are both actual and illusory. When we say that there are three vital considerations, we are speaking from the perspective of the path, rather than from the fruit or result—and in so doing we are dividing an experience that

1. nga jyi'mèd (sNga phyi med), simultaneity.

actually is indivisible. This has to be explained before we can move on to attempt to understand nyi'mèd—even though it may appear convoluted to divide a unitary experience purely in order to comprehend its unitary nature. As we come closer to the actual practice of Dzogchen, paradox becomes increasingly the default medium of communication.

We need to be clear from the beginning that we are making this division in order to define methods of practice, according to the intricacies of a dualized mind-set. From the standpoint of dualism, these practice considerations are divided in order to define that which is not divided—in terms of our dualistic experience of practice. The fact that we discern these divisions both defines what is meant by the term *dualistic condition*[2] and provides the methodology for realizing nonduality.

The natural development of lha-tong takes us into the stage known as nyi'mèd. Nyi'mèd means "indivisibility."[3] It is with the practice of nyi'mèd that we approach nonduality and arrive at the threshold of the practice of Dzogchen. With nyi'mèd, what is sought is the lack of difference between the quality of the experience of emptiness and the quality of the experiences of form: space and energy, absence of namthogs and movement of namthogs, mi-thogpa and *thogpa*. These experiences need to be discovered as having one taste.[4] We need to find ourselves in the condition in which we are not distracted from presence of awareness, either by mental events or by their absence.

It is actually not possible to practice nyi'mèd—at a certain stage of practice, nyi'mèd simply happens. It happens when we find ourselves moving without design between the states of shi-nè and lha-tong. This natural movement simply presents itself, of itself[5]—as soon as one finds the presence of awareness in the dimensions of mi-thogpa (or nè-pa) and gYo-wa.

From the perspective of Dzogchen, the states of nè-pa and gYo-wa are both artificial because they are partial experiences. It is only when

2. nyi-su ma-wa (gNyis su sMra ba), dualism or dualistic condition.
3. gNyis med, undivided. Nyi is "two" and med is "not."
4. ro-chig (ro gCig), one taste.
5. thamal rang 'dro (tha mal rang 'gros), natural movement.

both are free to manifest that the uncontrived nature of reality can be said to be present. Having found one's awareness nonseparate in the presence of that uncontrived nature, one can then experience the one taste of emptiness and form.

The actual experience, however, may not be so immediately accessible, and one may have to spend a long time merely experiencing the alternation of nè-pa and gYo-wa. The one taste of nè-pa and gYo-wa cannot be sought. One cannot actually practice nyi'mèd. However, one can be open to the possibility of experiencing the one taste—and that in itself is nyi'mèd. From this perspective, nyi'mèd is simply the capacity to dwell in either mi-thogpa or gYo-wa.

QUESTIONS AND ANSWERS

QUESTION: You mentioned two paired sets of words: the absence of namthogs as distinct from the movement of namthogs, and mi-thogpa as distinct from thogpa. It would seem as if namthog and thogpa mean the same thing?

NGAKPA CHÖGYAM RINPOCHE: That could be said, yes. But it depends upon the context in which these words are used. In Sanskrit, thogpa is *vitarka* and namthog is *vikalpa*, but actually that is not very helpful when it comes to the discussion of Dzogchen Sem-dé. The meaning of these words in Sanskrit carries the sense in which they're used within the Sutras. When we use the word *namthog* in terms of finding the presence of awareness in the movement of namthogs, we are using the word *namthog* as a contraction of the term *namthog gomdu charwa*,[6] which means "thought arising as meditation." So when we say "absence of namthogs" having the same taste as the "movement of namthogs," this relates with empty presence and thought arising as meditation. This relates more with nyi'mèd. When we say mi-thogpa has the same taste as thogpa, this relates more with the movement between shi-nè and lha-tong. It's a highly subtle and technical distinction, though.

6. rNam rTog bsGom du 'char ba.

KHANDRO DÉCHEN: Yes—and it's not so important to be quite so involved with these terms.

NCR: Quite—that's more the academic aspect of the field.

Q: I'm grateful for the answer nonetheless, particularly the clarification of *namthog* as a contraction of the term *namthog gomdu charwa*. Somehow the definition is highly provocative. "Thought arising as meditation"—that really defines a central aspect of Dzogchen, or have I missed the point?

NCR: No. That *is* the very point of what we are discussing together.

KD: And *that* could happen at any moment.

CHAPTER 10

The Dimension of
Nongradual Approach

*The perspective of Dzogchen is always that we are all enlight-
ened from beginninglessness. Because of this, inspiration is possible. Inspiration is the power of the enlightened state to make
itself known: to itself, through itself, and of itself. A synapse
can occur in which we glimpse, for a moment or an eternity, the
manifest nakedness of being.*

THIS IS the final phase of a journey that never began. Because it
had no inception, it has no cessation. This final phase is essentially a continuous simultaneity. We began with linear concepts—but
through the experience of the journey, those concepts, valuable as
they were when the journey was a journey, have now become obso-
lete. In this phase, inception and culmination cannot be distinguished
beyond the sheer presence[1] of their dissolution into each other. It is a
journey into vastness.

Before we go any further with our discussion of what is meant by
the term *nongradual practice*, we need to review the nature of what we
have been evolving as a gradualist construct. We have spent some time

1. sel-nang (gSal sNang), sheer presence.

developing a sequence of images. At one level, these images have provided an imaginal structure that relates to what appears to be real in terms of meditational experience. We have constructed a traveler's guide that provides possible routes into what may at first have seemed to be an unmapped region. That is obviously a matter of excitement for those who find themselves moved by the possibilities offered by Vajrayana. But we cannot remain with this image—exciting, beautiful, or otherwise. It is a good map, and one upon which we may occasionally have need to rely, but at some point we have to dispense with the linear constructs that took us beyond the edge of what we previously knew.

We have looked at the first three of the series of practices known as the Four Naljors: shi-nè, lha-tong, and nyi'mèd. The final practice is known as lhun-drüp, but before we discuss lhun-drüp, we need to examine the meaning of the Four Naljors and the context within which it exists as a method. The word *naljor* means "remaining in the natural state." Naljor is a contraction of the words *nalma* and *jorpa*.[2] *Nalma* means "natural," and *jorpa* means "remaining." Since the word *naljor* is used within the Tantras to translate the word *yoga*, it is important to distinguish its unique usage in Dzogchen terminology. In the Tantras, *naljor* means union or unification, whereas in Dzogchen it means "remaining in the natural state."

The Four Naljors are the ngöndro, or principal means of entry, into the practice of Sem-dé—the nature of Mind series of Dzogchen.[3] The Four Naljors presented here belong to the visionary teaching cycles of Aro Lingma, which are known as the Aro gTér, or visionary treasures of Aro.[4] However, these practices can also be found

2. rNal ma and 'byor pa.
3. The actual practice of Dzogchen Sem-dé is called the Four Ting-ngé'dzins (meditative absorptions, or samadhis). These comprise of nè-pa (undisturbed), mi-gYo-wa (unmoving), nyam-nyid (undivided) and lhun-drüp (uninhibited spontaneity).
4. Kyungchen Aro Lingma ('khyung chen A ro gLing ma), 1886–1923, was a female Nyingma gTértön (discoverer of visionary revelation teachings).

within other lineages of the Nyingma tradition and within the Kagyüd schools, where they are known as Formless Mahamudra.[5]

Apart from lhun-drüp, these four terms are not unique to Dzogchen, so it is necessary to establish the distinction between the way in which they are used in the different contexts of Sutra, Tantra, and Dzogchen. It is not our purpose here to classify these distinctions in detail, but we will give a general picture in order to describe the manner in which the Four Naljors function as an independent meditational approach.

The first two Naljors, shi-nè and lha-tong, are practiced extensively within the Sutric teachings—but not in the same style or from the same perspective as we have described here. Shamatha and vipashyana, as they are spoken of in Sutra, are similar to shi-nè and lha-tong as they are discussed in Dzogchen Sem-dé—but they are not nondual in the nature of their application.[6] The first three Naljors—shi-nè, lha-tong, and nyi'mèd—are terms used in Tantra but, again, not in the same way as they are used in Dzogchen Sem-dé. In Tantra, these terms are linked with visualization and, although the idea of unifying emptiness and form is present, there is the sense in which they must be unified. The principle by which they are simply recognized as nondual is particular to Dzogchen. The final Naljor, lhun-drüp, applies only to the Dzogchen teachings.

The first three Naljors have been described as a progressive series of practices culminating in the practice of nyi'mèd. We explored these in the previous chapter, but we will list them again briefly in order to provide the clearest context for what we are about to present.

5. Also called the Four Naljors of Mahamudra. Shi-nè equates with tsé-chig (rTse gCig), one-pointedness; lha-tong equates with trö-dral (sPros 'bral), freedom from conceptual elaborations; nyi'mèd equates with ro-chig (ro gCig), one taste; and lhun-drüp equates with gom-mèd (sGom med), nonmeditation.

6. It should be noted here that *shamatha* and *vipashyana* are simply the Sanskrit words of which *shi-nè* and *lha-tong* are the Tibetan equivalents. The Sanskrit words are employed here to indicate Sutric practices, whereas the Tibetan words are used to indicate Dzogchen practices.

- Shi-nè is the method of finding oneself in the space of Mind without content while maintaining presence of awareness.
- Lha-tong is the method of reintegrating the presence of awareness with the movement of whatever arises in Mind.
- Nyi'mèd is the recognition of ro-chig, the one taste of emptiness and form.[7]

These three practices establish the ground for integration. Once we have experience of these practices, Dzogchen can become a reality. Before they are known at a personal experiential level, any concept of Dzogchen as a practice can have little meaning other than as a source of inspiration. For anyone who is still attempting to establish the base for practicing Dzogchen, the main purpose of discussing Dzogchen is to provide inspiration. The perspective of Dzogchen is always that we are all enlightened from beginninglessness. Because of this, inspiration is possible. Inspiration is the power of the enlightened state to make itself known: to itself, through itself, and of itself. A synapse can occur in which we glimpse, for a moment or an eternity, the manifest nakedness of being.[8]

We now have some experience of shi-nè and lha-tong. We have also "finger-painted" some indication as to what nyi'mèd might be. But what of lhun-drüp? Can we even point in the direction of lhun-drüp? Before we can say anything about lhun-drüp, we need to reassess the manner in which the practices have unfolded according to our presentation up to this point. We therefore suggest that, having read this far, it would also be useful to sit.

EXERCISE 9

Sit comfortably with your eyes wide open. Remain alert but without tension.

---

7. The energy that arises and dissolves within the spaciousness of being.
8. jen-par shar-wa (rJen par shar ba), nakedness.

FOLLOW UP EXERCISE 9

This exercise is similar both to the concluding exercises in the previous chapter and to exercise 1 in chapter 2. This is a deliberate device on our part. It is designed to clarify certain points in an experiential manner: We begin with mind as thought. We discover Mind without thought. We return to thought as Mind.

Kyabjé Chhi'mèd Rig'dzin Rinpoche once asked me [Ngakpa Chögyam] a question while we were sitting together in a small garden in Holland. He pointed up into the branches of the old apple tree in whose shade we sat. "In your experiencing," he asked, "which is moving—the leaves or the wind?" He was wearing the impassive and acutely observant expression that I had come to know quite well over the years. I knew what this meant. His question was intended to rip my understanding apart and expose whether there was any substance to it. He had asked me questions like this before, and I knew that it was only my immediate answer that interested him. If I took too long thinking about it, he would no longer be interested in hearing my reply. "It's my mind which moves, Rinpoche," I answered rather sheepishly, at which he smiled very slightly and said, "Maybe you hear this question before?" I said that I had not heard the question before, but that it seemed to have the same flavor as what Kyabjé Chatral Rinpoche had once said about phenomena: "Is it phenomena which move, or the mind which perceives them?" He looked at me intently for a second and then we both burst out laughing.

Movement within emptiness characterizes the nature of both Mind and reality. Realization is the reintegration of presence of awareness with whatever arises as the experience of being. In a certain sense, it is not completely possible to present the Four Naljors in a linear manner because our experience does not necessarily conform to the linear model. Let us look at what this means. If you are practicing shi-nè and you experience the arising and dissolution of thought into emptiness, what can you say about that experience? If you continue with presence of awareness, then what is the difference between this state and the state of nyi'mèd? The answer could easily be "nothing at all." There is no reason that the state of nyi'mèd shouldn't be realized without passing through all the intervening stages. There is no reason it is not possible to move from shi-nè into lha-tong without having to pass through stabilized shi-nè. Fundamentally, stabilized shi-nè is more difficult to arrive at than lha-tong or nyi'mèd for some people. But without significant experience of stabilized shi-nè, the lha-tong and nyi'mèd experiences within shi-nè are mostly like lightning in a daytime sky. Enlightenment continually sparkles through. It sparkles through the unenlightenment that we continually fabricate from the ground of being. Because enlightenment continually sparkles through, anyone with or without meditative experience can have flashes of lha-tong or nyi'mèd experience.

Often, illness or a near-death experience can open us to such illuminating insights. Enlightenment *is* our natural state, and so it is not surprising that it manifests from time to time. Unenlightenment is the constant activity in which we engage. We have to work at it all the time. So when life circumstances intervene, in terms of short-circuiting this continual effort, we experience glimpses of realization. These glimpses can radically change people's lives, but it is a hit-or-miss affair to hope that life is going to "do it for you" when the time is ripe. You have to cooperate with the sparkling-through of enlightenment by disengaging from referentiality and continuing with presence of awareness.

So it is not possible to say that the Naljors are a linear process, unless your experience also happens to evolve in a linear way. But although the process is not necessarily linear, it has to be described in that way. This kind of description operates in the same way that a series of words operates within a sentence. From the relative perspective, you cannot start with the meaning; you have to start with the first word of the sentence and proceed to the second, third, fourth, and so on. At the end of the sentence, the meaning becomes apparent. At the end of the sentence, the linearity of the words ceases to have any importance. Once you have read the sentence, you know its meaning. Once you know the meaning, you can, if you wish, return to the individual words in any particular order according to what you feel is appropriate.

Lhun-drüp is our spontaneous self-perfectedness. It is the fourth Naljor. Lhun-drüp is the knowledge that is there at the end of the sentence. If we forget, or get distracted from the meaning of the sentence, we may have to review the word order again. Lhun-drüp is the integration of the experience of nyi'mèd with every aspect of being. We move beyond practice. There is no method with lhun-drüp apart from continuing in the nondual presence of awareness in the efflorescence of every moment.

QUESTIONS AND ANSWERS

QUESTION: I've heard you say that lha-tong included the *Paramitas*. Could you elaborate on that?

NGAKPA CHÖGYAM RINPOCHE: Definitely. The Ten Paramitas[9] are *jinpa*, generosity; *tsultrim*, honor; *zopa*, steadfastness; *tsöndru*, vitality; *samten*, meditative stability; *shérab*, knowledge or insight; *thab*, skillful means; *mönlam*, wish-path; *tob*, power or strength; and *yeshé*, primordial wisdom.[12] There are some of our own retranslations here, so I will give the more usual equivalents: *tsultrim* is more usually translated as ethical discipline, *zopa* as patience or tolerance, *tsöndru* as effort, and *mönlam* as prayer. So, let's look at lha-tong in this respect or, to be more accurate, let's look at the Four Naljors—because the *pa-rol tu chin-pa chu* actually apply to them all. If we start with shi-nè, generosity is vital if we are to give ourselves time to sit and if we are to give all sentient beings our time of sitting. We are not sitting in silence for ourselves; *that* is crucial. Generosity here means allowing space in which shi-nè can bring us into the experience of the empty state. In

9. pa-rol tu chin-pa chu (pha rol tu phyin pa bCu), Ten Paramitas.
10. sByin pa, tshul khrims, bZod pa, brTson 'grus, bSam gTan, shes rab, thabs, sMon lam, sTobs, ye shes.

lha-tong we have to have the generosity to allow namthogs to arise again—we are not going to remain in the selfish domain where thoughts are not welcome. In lha-tong we have to have the generosity to welcome whatever arises. Then we have tsultrim, or honor.

KHANDRO DÉCHEN: We prefer to use the term *honor* rather than *ethical discipline* because there are sometimes puritanical "religious" implications involved with ethical discipline. Honor means the same thing, but there's a sense of valor there. We have to be brave if we are to practice shi-nè, and we have to be brave if we are to practice lha-tong. We have to be brave if we are to stare into the face of emptiness and form and find the presence of rigpa. Honor means doing what one says one will do. It means sitting when one doesn't particularly want to sit. It means persisting in one's practice and not being seduced by other alternatives. Then there's zopa—steadfastness. *Patience* and *tolerance* are also valuable words. Maybe zopa is only adequately expressed by the three together. When one practices shi-nè, one needs to be steadfast. To practice shi-nè might be to be bored out of your mind. To practice the Tantric ngöndro you might experience physical pain, and you will certainly experience frustration.

NCR: Patience goes without saying, then. One has to manifest patience with the seemingly endless stream of thought and the seemingly endless series of repetitive movements. If one is impatient, there's no hope. Patience arises out of generosity. One has been generous. One has said, "Here—this time is given for all beings." What can one do then but manifest patience? What else can one do but experience the results of generosity with tolerance? Whatever happens, happens. We have agreed to that. We've given the ground. We've allowed the theater of phenomenal reality to open. It's the first night. It's always the first night. The players are fresh and excited. The performance is magnificent. All that generosity floods back. One is patient as the play reveals itself. One is tolerant of whatever manifests.

KD: "Good thoughts," "bad thoughts"—they come and go, and one does not judge them. It's said that whether clouds are black or white, if they obscure the sun they are the same. This is the meaning of tolerance.

NCR: In the Tantric ngöndro, one has to have patience, acceptance, and tolerance. One has to be steadfast in the practice because many emotions begin to arise. There are always seemingly good reasons to give up the practice, but one perseveres. There is physical pain and apparent lack of result, but one continues all the same. Zopa. And then . . . what do we have next . . . tsöndru, vitality.

KD: The reason we don't use the word *effort* is that there is some sense of burden that seems to come across with that word. Vitality includes exertion and effort.

NCR: Vitality is the sense of being alive in one's practice. I'm not a dead body. One *is* alive. There is vitality in the practice. And, equally, one is alive in shi-nè and lha-tong.

KD: And then samten, meditative stability.

NCR: The stability of one's meditation is based upon the ground of generosity, patience, and vitality.

Q: How does all that lead to stability?

NCR: Generosity is the space that allows everything to come and go, as we discussed previously. When phenomena are free to come and go, there is no instability because nothing has to be controlled. Likewise with patience—there is no neurotic hurry. The arising and dissolving can simply perform. With vitality, there is the sparkle of being present in all that—it's not merely a lethargic, stupefied, phlegmatic acceptance. Generosity, patience, and exertion equate with compassion, wisdom, and energy—the three important factors within Buddhist practice. In terms of Dzogchen, patience, vitality, and generosity are the three spheres of being: emptiness, energy, and form—chö-ku, long-ku, and trül-ku (dharmakaya, sambhogakaya, and nirmanakaya). So the samten Paramita is integral to the ngöndros of both Tantra and Dzogchen. Then there is shérab—knowledge or insight. Shérab simply comes about through one's involvement. There is no choice; flashes simply begin to occur. This is the point at which the experience of nyi'mèd percolates through the structure of the Tantric preliminaries. This is the point at which the preliminaries are no longer preliminaries and one begins to see that one could practice in this way for the rest of one's life.

This is what one could also call the purification of Dorje Sempa. Purification has different meanings according to the vehicle under discussion. In Dzogchen, the word relates to something that happens on its own. It means seeing it as pure because it already is pure. Here the word *pure* means "nondual," and the word *purification* pertains to a method of realizing the nondual state that has always been there. There is nothing to purify apart from the notion that there is something impure. Then there is thab, or skillful means. This is the point at which we recognize that these practices really are the heart of the matter. The flashes of shérab have made this possible, and now we see what we can do. We begin to see that something is possible. We see that we are personally involved in a process from which there's no turning back. We begin to see that the method is really, actually directly connected with where we are. These ngöndros are no longer Tibetan practices. They are part of what we are and what we are becoming. And then mönlam—wish-path or aspiration.

KD: One could translate *mönlam* as "the direction of aspiration" or "aspirational direction." Obviously, when we see what is possible, we have no choice in what we do. Our own liberation seems possible, and so the liberation of all other beings begins to gain the momentum of inevitability.

Questions and Answers

Physical Openness

QUESTION: There are those who might be disturbed at the prospect of sitting meditation, especially if they feel physically challenged by the posture. Could you address this issue?

KHANDRO DÉCHEN: Simply sitting and being where we are should be easy, but apparently it's not. Being out of balance with ourselves can turn sitting into a monumental effort. One could find the simplicity of sitting an almost impossible battle against restlessness, irritation, and drowsiness.

NGAKPA CHÖGYAM RINPOCHE: Yes, it's pertinent to remember that. Really—in order to develop the practice of shi-nè, one needs to encourage body knowledge. We need to physically remember the state of natural equipoise and balance.

KD: The first factor to remember concerning sitting is that you need to be comfortable. The main barrier to comfortable sitting is the idea that one requires backrests or walls upon which to lean. People tend to have ideas about comfort that often inhibit natural comfort and ease. The part of the body that usually gets the worst treatment from these ideas is the spine. Learning to be comfortable is an art—an art in which one is encouraging one's own body knowledge.

Q: Being comfortable is important to me because it's no help at all if my body (and specifically my back) is causing me painful distraction.

NCR: It's crucial not to be distracted by your physical posture. But this doesn't mean that we should lose all body awareness and disappear into some heady region in which we're removed from the blood, flesh, sinew, skin, and bone of what we are.

Q: Khandro Déchen, you said that the crucial factor according to the practice of the Four Naljors is that the spine should sit naturally. Is there more you could say about that?

KD: The posture should help us to be both relaxed and alert. You need to be both relaxed *and* alert, and so lying down would be problematic. Lying down might be comfortable, but drowsiness or sleep might easily result. A good upright chair can be useful for sitting as long as it keeps the thighs and spine at ninety degrees to each other. Using a chair of this type should not be considered a concession to age. Anyone can sit in a chair, no matter what age one happens to be—the position is as worthy as any other. Any padded upright chair is good. When the spine is in its natural position it just *sits there* and the pelvis settles comfortably around it—there's no effort at all involved in sitting upright, and that's ideal for shi-nè. But it's not always possible to have a chair. If you're traveling, out in the countryside, or in a group, you'll need other ways of sitting.

NCR: It's valuable to look at the traditional postures for practice, not only because they're received through transmission but also because they give you a broader range of options. People have to experiment on an individual basis in order to find out what lies within the scope of their own capacities.

Q: I think most people who begin to practice shi-nè immediately assume that they should sit with their legs crossed.

NCR: Yes—unfortunately this can almost be guaranteed to make people feel that shi-nè is an alien practice, designed for people from Eastern countries who were brought up to sit in such a manner.

KD: If you just sit on a cushion and cross your legs, your body is invariably going to become a painful distraction. Sitting on any normal type of cushion with your legs crossed will cause your knees to be higher than your hips. This causes two distinct problems. First, the alignment of the legs makes the pelvis tilt backward and creates an unstable seat for the spine. In practical terms, this means that when you sit in this way, one of two things must happen: either you'll slouch forward and get a backache (and drowsiness) or you'll try to straighten your back. The constant effort of keeping your back straight will also give you a backache, but it will be combined with tension and fatigue. Even if you lean against a wall (which is regarded as unseemly in the Tibetan tradition) the same problems will arise, albeit to a lesser extent. Second, the effect of your knees being higher than your hips gives you intense pins and needles in your legs. If you ignore your legs' going to sleep, then you'll experience difficulty when you try to stand up again at the end of your sitting session, until you've gone through several minutes of pain. This posture is unstable and will be one of the worst obstacles to practice you'll encounter as you set out on this path. In order to adjust your posture to eliminate such problems, you'll need to raise your buttocks high enough from the ground to allow your knees to fall below the level of your hips—it's that simple.

Temporal Openness

Q: Wouldn't it be useful if we were able to give up other involvements and concentrate on practice?

KD: No—probably not.

NCR: Right. You see, the view of Dzogchen in particular is one of integration, and that view is particularly pertinent for the West at this time. Becoming a real practitioner is not necessarily about giving up relationships, home, and job in order to disappear into the mountains of India or Nepal—no matter how spiritually romantic that may seem. We are advocating an escape *into* reality, rather than an escape *from* it.

KD: The problem of how to develop your practice beyond a certain threshold is one that we all face at some point. Some of you *may* decide to curtail your social lives, or abandon them altogether in favor of intense practice, but that's sometimes not altogether helpful. I'm generally not in favor of extremism—rather, I'm enthusiastic about the possibility of anyone and everyone being able to integrate this kind of practice into their lives.

NCR: But this still leaves the problem of time and the fact that there never seems to be quite enough of it.

KD: If you want to take your practice further without disengaging from life as it's usually lived in society, you can either accept your situation and allow your experience of practice to develop at its own rate—or you can engage in periodic retreats.

NCR: Accepting your limitations in terms of daily practice is by no means to be underrated as a way of living and growing as a human being. We have seen too many people take on too much in the way of practice only to let the whole thing fall apart at some later stage because they were living in some fantasy world. It's easy to want to be great practitioners—we can all have such desires, obsessions, or inspirations—but if you cannot be yourself and practice at *that*, you may not realize anything at all.

Q: So how do I push through the stuckness of feeling that my level of experience is not moving anywhere?

NCR: In order to break through plateaus of experience that you've come to relate to as barriers to the expansiveness of your sitting, you can go on retreat. The Tibetan word *tsam*,[1] which is usually rendered as "retreat," actually means "confines." The idea is that you establish the *confines* in which you practice. Retreat can be solitary or entered into in groups. Retreat can last an hour, a day, a week, a month, a year, three years, or any of these measures. Retreats can be open or closed—you can either be in touch with the outside world or completely cut off from it for the extent of your retreat. So with any re-

1. mTshams.

treat, you establish what the confines are going to be—and then you abide by that decision.

KD: Sitting with a group of people is a supportive experience and one that will strengthen your individual practice. Spending time with a group of people with shared commitment to practice can have a significant effect on your continued personal practice. The idea of spiritual nourishment becomes more vital as you proceed with practice, and as you do so it becomes valuable to dedicate yourself to the thought of nourishing others. When you've recognized the necessity of extending the warmth you are discovering to others, you should allow and encourage yourself to be continually moved by that intention. In this spirit, you can dedicate the development of your own practice to the liberation of everyone who has become distracted from their beginningless enlightenment. Although, ultimately, you are alone on this path and have to operate from that solitary peak, relatively, we can all help one another. Being able to share experiences with other practitioners in workshops and learning from one another's unique perspectives is something quite valuable.

But then there are silent group retreats in which you can engage in more intensive practice. Group retreat can be a powerful experience in which you can support each other through your natural warmth, your presence, and your stillness. To be *with* others, without verbal communication, is to open up to other levels of communication that function in terms of sharing time and space. It's always easier to maintain your practice when you practice with others, and so this kind of group retreat can make for breakthrough experiences that can radically shift the emphasis of your daily sitting. It's crucial, however, that you don't grasp at these changes or try to solidify them into possessions or definitions of who you are.

NCR: Group retreats are a good basis for solitary retreats. Solitary retreats are by far the most intense kind of practice and certainly the strongest method of transforming your notions of what you are. But it's not wise to go into solitary retreat too quickly, or the experience may be either disappointing or too threatening.

KD: It may be difficult to find anyone to give you the guidance you need, and so we will lay down some rough guidelines for anyone who feels confident enough of their sitting practice to engage in solitary retreat. Short retreats can be accommodated in your own home, but longer retreats need to be entered into at a retreat center where your food can be properly organized and where there's the possibility of asking for guidance from a Lama or meditation instructor with the appropriate experience.

NCR: We would not recommend that anyone engage in a solitary retreat for longer than one weekend.

KD: Yes—and don't try to sit beyond your physical capacity to sit. If you're only used to sitting for an hour a day, then any length of retreat is bound to put a strain on your legs. So be kind to yourself and don't push yourself beyond your limits. Generally speaking, people have two kinds of limits—a soft limit and a hard limit. If you don't push yourself beyond your soft limit, you'll never get anywhere. But if you try to push yourself beyond your hard limit, you'll damage yourself and become disenchanted with the whole idea. This is all part of developing your awareness. It's fine to endure a little pain in the legs, but you need to be in touch with the point at which determination stops and masochism starts. If you enter into retreat prematurely, you might never want to try it again—and that would be a shame.

Q: It seems very important to get enough experience of solitary retreat, and I'd like to know how to do that. It seems an ideal way to get practice off to a good start. It seems like I could break through a lot of barriers that way.

NCR: It's not wise to go into solitary retreat too quickly or the experience may put you off for life! It's not really worth going into solitary retreat without the advice of a teacher, and most Buddhist centers with retreat facilities insist that you have the permission of a teacher in order to enter into retreat. You may find that you need to have an interview with the spiritual director of the center at which you intend to enter into retreat, so that it can be established that you are properly prepared. This isn't very surprising, because in other fields the same principle applies. You need to log so many hours of flying with an instructor before you can get your pilot's license and fly solo. So, to fly solo in solitary retreat and for it to be a creative experience, you'll need to prepare properly and be able to process your experiences in a way that will be beneficial. A teacher can comment on many facets of these experiences in a way that enriches your life as a practitioner.

Q: You said that you wouldn't recommend that anyone engage in a solitary retreat for longer than one weekend. Could you say a little more about that? What kind of time would a weekend retreat cover?

NCR: Friday night till Monday morning.

Q: And if I wanted to do longer?

NCR: You shouldn't really do that without seeking advice—and you should get the advice as near as possible to the time of the retreat.

KD: Even before attempting a weekend solitary retreat of this kind, we'd strongly advise going on a few silent group retreats. Much may be accomplished through quite short retreats, such as one-day or half-day retreats. A half-day retreat would start after lunch and finish the following morning, the night having been passed sleeping in the retreat room. A day retreat would begin an hour or so before going to sleep, continue through the following day and finish an hour or so after waking the day after. These extra hour periods before and after should be used for starting and completing the retreat with practice. There should be very little in the room to distract you, and you should avoid taking in any reading matter. The practices in which you engage should be those outlined in this book, interspersed with walking meditation or light exercise. Meditative walking is very slow and deliberate, and as you walk you should find the presence of your awareness in the movements of your body.

Ambient Time

Q: Can I ask you about time as it relates to practice? I want to enter into this practice and make the Four Naljors part of my life.

KD: You'll need to observe how you are and how you structure your day. You'll need to look at how you use your time. You'll also need to give some attention to how you feel at different periods throughout the day. This is quite personal. We're all different. There's no set formula that suits everyone. If we were to give some kind of rigid rule about the best time to sit, it might be excellent for some people but possibly counterproductive for others. The most important point is that you discover for yourself how to use your time in the most skillful way.

As a general principle, first thing in the morning is an excellent time for sitting. But if you're one of those people who come alive at night, this advice may well be rather off-putting. Two possible alternatives arise if you're a seminocturnal person: Either you can readjust your body clock (gently and gradually over the course of a few months) or you can accept how you are and discover your own best time. It's worth trying to adjust your body clock, though, because being misaligned with the natural cycle of darkness and light tends to deplete the life force. Being awake during too many hours of darkness and sleeping during too many hours of daylight puts your energy out of balance. It can lead to depression and irritability—a fact worth bearing in mind if you work night shifts. You actually *need* to see full-spectrum sunlight in order to remain lively and bright. If you're a night worker, it's a good idea to obtain full-spectrum lighting in your home so that you don't suffer too much light deprivation. But whatever your circumstances, you must respect and work with how you are rather than attempting to force anything. If it's too difficult to sit early in the morning, then you'll probably get little out of it, and if you get little out of your sitting, you'll probably give it up. So it's better to sit when you feel fresh and alert. Sitting first thing in the morning is usually recommended because it's a unique juncture in our daily stream of experience. The time when you wake up is quite special because, although you may well have been conceptualizing wildly in the dream state, at least there's been a break from the habitual patterns of waking conceptuality. At the point of waking, there's no accumulation of "today's conceptual patterns." The time of waking is an opening between two long tracts of crowdedness. If you can simply *be* in this openness, that is in itself meditation. Allowing this sense of spaciousness to become increasingly expansive is something that happens more naturally on waking.

NCR: But getting up in the morning is not always so easy for people. One of the chief difficulties of getting up is the blurring that occurs in the transition between waking and getting out of bed. Once you find yourself in that blurred state, it's highly likely to become protracted unless you have some pressing reason to rouse yourself. The main problem is that this blurring can feel like a luxuriously comfortable state. A lot of people find it difficult to accept that remaining in this blurred, drowsy state is undesirable. Usually, when we talk about it in negative terms, people become rather anxious and summon up all kinds of defenses. They often tell us that they need that time of drowsing in order to feel fully rested. We often reply, "That's like saying you need to remain tense in order to relax." People are often quite surprised to hear that this blurred drowse is in fact most unrestful. It leaves you bereft of the freshness you could experience by waking and getting up in a sharper, clearer, and more distinct way. The *only* way to get up skillfully is to get up immediately on waking. Gradual waking up drains your energy and often leaves you feeling as if you could use another night's sleep. It's in this blurred, drowsy state that you get the most bizarre and frustrating dreams—dreams that are continually disturbed by figments of wakefulness. Dream consciousness intrudes on waking consciousness and waking consciousness intrudes on dream consciousness. Buddhist practice is geared toward *waking up*. Linking the practice of waking from the sleep of misapprehension with waking from nightly sleep is a powerful coincidence in the development of practice. Anything that can be done to enhance presence and alertness is valuable.

KD: A quick facial wash and vigorous rub dry can be most helpful first thing in the morning, but it's good to leave as little time as possible between waking and sitting. If it's cold, it's a good idea to wrap yourself in a warm blanket. Try to avoid turning up the heat, because sitting in a stuffy, overheated room will make you drowsy. It might even send you off to sleep again!

NCR: Many people find it good to have a meditation shawl, which they keep specifically for their practice and which they use for no other purpose. Maroon or red is a good color for such a wrap.[2] According to the Tibetan Buddhist tradition, red is the color of energy, and a certain quiet and relaxed energy is required in order to remain alert in practice. The early Buddhist schools wore yellow as the color of practice, because yellow is the color of purity. But there came a time when Buddhism was under attack from those who followed paths of philosophical extremism.[3] It was at that time that Padmasambhava decided it was necessary to wear red robes as an outer symbol of strength in practice. This was also a consideration in terms of the fact that the Tirthikas had adopted yellow as the color of their clothing. Originally, the color of Buddhist robes came from the sulfurous stream in which the first articles of monks' clothing were washed. Shakyamuni Buddha's disciples asked him what they should wear, and he replied that they should collect rags from the village midden and wash them in the nearby stream. These rags should then be sewn together and worn as robes. The sulfurous stream dyed the rags yellow, and thus the tradition of yellow robes was established. When the tradition was taken to Tibet, the only economically available red dye was made from a variety

2. Red, rather than maroon, is the color that is used in the Aro gTér lineage. Aro Lingma advised a return to the original red color recommended by Padmasambhava. Red is also the color of the solar channel.
3. The philosophical extremists were called Tirthikas, and they espoused views of either monism, dualism, nihilism, or eternalism.

of grass that produced a brown shade of maroon, and this has now become the traditional color of Tibetan Buddhist robes. The exception to this is the Gélug school, who, under Jé Tsongkhapa, moved back to the use of yellow on the basis that times had changed. It was perceived that there was a need for purity of practice rather than energy in counteracting hostile influences.

KD: Using colors and connecting with them through the visual faculties is a method of creating conducive circumstances for the development of energy at the level of practice. The more care and sensitivity you put into your practice equipment, the more it will generate the *feel* of the time when you can sit and be. The shawl, like the block, cushion, or stool, will become wonderfully familiar to you as you continue in your practice. The care with which you handle these things and pack them away after use will also become part of your practice. Objects treated in this way will become valuable supports for practice in their own right, and when using them you'll find yourself more able to enter into the spirit of practice.

Q: I get concerned about my capacity when people tell me they're sitting for an hour or more every day . . . is it worth sitting for short periods of time?

KD: It's good to sit for a length of time that you can manage every day. Don't be tempted to sit for longer than you are really able. If you do, you'll just end up finding excuses for not sitting every day, and then you'll feel as if you've failed. It's vital to develop confidence rather than creating a sense of incompetence and failure. So proceed at your own speed. If you sit for five minutes every day and actually let go and let be—that could easily be better than the accomplishment of those who consider themselves to be meditative long-termers. However long you or other people sit, it's not a competition. Or if it is, it's not practice. Don't make promises to yourself that you cannot keep, or you'll end up not being able to keep promises to yourself about anything. Start with what you can do easily, and promise your-self that you'll sit for that length of time every day. It's better to sit for five or ten minutes a day than for an hour every once in a while. Daily practice is vital, and until you can establish a daily practice, you'll find it difficult to enter fully into the experience of sitting. Sitting has to become part of the natural flow and pattern of your life or it will al-ways be something "special." This may seem a strange thing to say in view of the many special things we have said about it, but the spe-cialness of sitting cannot be found outside its ordinariness. Until you sit every day, sitting will never become ordinary, and if it never be-comes ordinary, it will never be special. The special quality of sitting is something that should not be limited to the time in which you sit. Sitting that has this special quality permeates the rest of your day, giv-ing you access to a more spacious sense of being. Beyond the formal pattern of your everyday sitting, it's valuable to utilize other moments that happen to make themselves available to you. During the day, it's often possible to enter the momentary openings between activities in which you can stop—to let go and let be. This momentary practice of letting go and letting be infuses your daily life experience with a sense of openness—you become more able to *see* how you cause your own confusion and frustration.

NCR: Daily sitting is the base for other moments of openness dur-ing each day. These moments can occur in bus queues—

KD: —they can occur on trains or while making love, walking in the hills, swimming in the sea, or lying on the beach . . .

NCR: There are no limits to this openness. Moments such as these are infinite, and once we find ourselves within them, we become open to the infinite nature of what we are.

KD: The place you choose to sit is also significant—because, ulti-mately, although it can be anywhere, relatively, the place and its at-mosphere have an effect on you. Not everyone can have a special room set aside for the sole purpose of sitting. It's useful to make ready some place in your house or flat where you can sit and feel it's where you should be. It's not really conducive to sit among careless heaps of accumulated household paraphernalia.

NCR: If you just sit anywhere without any sensitivity to your environment, then you'll create an untidy energy within yourself. It's possible to sit anywhere and under any prevailing conditions, but for that you need to have *ultimate view*. As long as you only have relative view, some situations are conducive and others, nonconducive. If the place where you sit reflects your distraction rather than your attuned intent toward realization, the atmosphere of your practice will be restricted in its conduciveness to opening.

KD: It's necessary to be generous with respect to the practice in which you're engaging. It's also necessary to respect your own intention. If you invite someone to your home because you're strongly attracted to the person and you'd like to get a romantic liaison going, then you need to create conducive circumstances.

NCR: If this person is the subject of appreciable desire, and you want to succeed in your seduction—there's no purpose to inviting him or her back to a scene of rank squalor. Nothing is served by the offer of sharing a tin of beans on burned toast served up on chipped, greasy plates that have been pulled out of a cluster of unwashed mess in the sink. You don't leave the fire down so low that you both have to keep your overcoats on and sit half-blinded by the stark lightbulb dangling unshaded in the middle of the room.

Q: But some people live on limited resources . . .

KD: Yes, but no matter how poor you are, you can put some care and effort into making your environment pleasant. The Tibetan refugees in the Himalayas, no matter how poor they are, always make their home environment clean and attractive. They paper the packed mud walls of their houses with newspaper and, when possible, with color supplements or *National Geographic* magazines. They paint tin cans and use them as plant pots and generally make the best of whatever little they have.

NCR: There's always a sense of both openness and color in Tibetan homes—a feeling of natural nobility. So, even if you're socially deprived and unable to alter your circumstances due to the policies of corrupt and inhumane regimes, you can still liberate the expression of your innate human dignity. Living like a slob even if you happen to be monumentally wealthy is nonconducive to the *atmosphere* of practice. In the Tibetan tradition, practitioners employ all manner of complex sensory devices and imagery in order to create conducive circumstances for practice. We're not saying that people need to build their own Tibetan temple before they start to sit, or even that they should have a special room—but some effort should be made in recognition of the nature of the practice in which you wish to involve yourself.

Q: Yes, I've found that having some focus in my place of sitting is valuable, like having a picture that inspires me to practice.

KD: Yes—to be able to open your eyes and gaze nonconceptually on the awareness-image of Padmasambhava or Yeshé Tsogyel as a focus is considered very helpful.

Q: But wouldn't this mean that you'd think about the awareness-image or generate some kind of attitude toward it?

KD: No, you should just let the focus of your eyes soften a little and simply wordlessly gaze until the buzz of thoughts has calmed a little. In order to create conducive circumstances, you may like to light a candle or a night-light—a stick of incense might also enhance the atmosphere for practice.

Q: None of these things are ultimately necessary though, are they?

KD: No—but because of the ritual quality of our lives, engaging in *creative ritual* can facilitate an attitude conducive to openness. Considering the ultimate and relative views of supports for practice, it's important not to seduce yourself with the idea of the ultimate. Sometimes people may like to imagine that they can operate from an ultimate perspective, but unless they really find themselves in that view through their developed openness, they'll just end up depriving themselves of support and inspiration. Any practice functions in terms of time, place, and person, and what is practical when those factors are seen in context with each other. Once you have an exact idea of how to enter into practice, you can examine your situation and work out what's possible. You can observe yourself and become sensitive to what fits with your unique circumstances.

Q: You said that meditating for five minutes every day if you did it in the right way could be better than sitting for an hour or more. But I've often been told that sitting for an hour a day was absolutely necessary and that the length of sitting periods was a crucial factor.

NCR: It's obviously valuable to sit for an hour a day. The reason we stress the quality of the sitting period rather than the duration is that some people simply go through the motions of sitting. Being able to sit for an hour a day is certainly a "discipline"—and that *is* valuable. But what if you come to resent that discipline? What happens if you don't have time to sit for a full hour every day? What happens if your emotional situation becomes intense and an hour of sitting becomes painful or claustrophobic? Some people sit for their hour and drowse. Some people sit for their hour and daydream. Some people alternate between drowsing and drifting through vague patterns of thought.

Q: But in zazen someone comes around with a stick to keep you alert and reminds you of what you're really supposed to be doing.

NCR: Yes. That's valuable. But what happens when you sit on your own? What about when there's no one to remind you of your discipline?

Attuned Intent

Q: I've always been very interested and impressed by Buddhism and what it has to tell us about reality; I can't imagine a superior outlook on life—but I can't seem to find time for meditation. I want to meditate and I often promise myself I will get going with daily meditation, but then when I do get going it gets interrupted and I let weeks or months slip by. Can you give me some advice on this?

NCR: How much do you *want* to practice?

Q: It's very important to me.

NCR: That's interesting. I wonder why *that* is? [*pause*] Let me see if I understand you correctly. You *want* to do something. It's *important* to *you*—but *you* don't do it. Have I understood you correctly? Was that the gist of what you said?

Q: Yes.

NCR: Well, the answer is fairly simple then. When you want to meditate more than you want to use your free time in other ways, you'll find less difficulty. I must apologize if that sounds somewhat blunt, but it's a simple statement of the manner in which motivation functions. We could look at it another way. What if I told you, "I want to get thinner, but I keep eating too much and don't exercise." Your response might be the same: "You obviously like eating and not exercising more than you'd like to be thinner."

KD: We're not making a value judgment here either—we're just saying, "Enjoy the roundness of your belly as much as the taste of your food."

NCR: Or enjoy your moderation as much as your envisioned thinness.

Q: But isn't it important to meditate?

NCR: Of course . . . it's crucial [*laughs*]. But that's just us telling you that. What do *you* think? How important do *you* think it is?

Q: The Dharma books say—

NCR: Yes, "the Dharma books" say all kinds of things. People sometimes knock on our door and tell us what their book says—but what does that mean? What do *you* say?

Q: I guess I'm confused.

NCR: That's better! Splendid! That's a much better place to find yourself. The next step is to accept that with a certain sense of humor. No one enjoys confusion, but as long as we cling to our dualistic vision, we will always translate *not knowing* as "confusion." We don't like confusion because within the space of confusion definitions become vague and intangible. That makes us feel insecure. Accepting or relaxing in that insecurity is in itself a practice. This is the wisdom of insecurity. To be motivated, you have to develop your understanding of what the process of shi-nè helps you to discover. To develop motivation, you have to take a serious look at your life.

KD: It could also be humorous . . . seriously humorous.

NCR: Quite! [*laughs*]

KD: Not wanting to sit is not feeling motivated to change. Not feeling motivated to change is either being afraid of change or seeing no reason to change. If we have a good understanding of Buddhism through reading, reflecting, and listening—through checking these teachings against our own experience—motivation naturally develops. But take your time; be kind to yourself.

NCR: Be honest and question your present motivations accurately—allow your attuned intent to grow. This is your experiment, so you don't have to complicate it with guilt and frustration. You'll enter into practice when it makes sense at an experiential level. If we want to meditate because we think it's a religious observance, then real motivation may never arise from that.

KD: Accept yourself as you are, and start from there. How does that sound?

Q: It sounds like a big relief!

KD: If practice is a strong priority, we should avoid weakening it by letting our other priorities contend with it. So we should just sit. When we get home, we should sit. We should sit again tomorrow morning and continue sitting in that way. Every time we sit should be the first time, and every moment we live should be the last moment.

Remember to make friends with death, and let present sensations flow like sand slipping through your fingers. If you want to keep up a daily practice, you should make very sure that you really do want to sit every day—that it *is* important to you. Try to ensure that you make time and space available in your life for sitting, and avoid setting yourself up for failure.

Don't aim to sit for too long every day—keep a small promised time and don't increase it until you feel that you really need more sitting time to develop your practice. You can always sit beyond your promised time. Even if your promised time is only five minutes, it's far better to sit for five minutes a day than the odd half hour here and there. Only make promises to yourself that you know you can keep, otherwise you'll never have confidence in yourself and you'll find that you won't be able to make promises to yourself at all. Being able to make promises to yourself is keenly meaningful. It's a way of giving your life real direction and enabling something positive to happen—especially if you link your promises to the wish for the liberation of everyone everywhere. In this way, you can make sitting part of your life, and once it becomes part of your life, clarity will begin to develop. When you start to gain a little clarity, there will be a much stronger motivation to practice. Once you see the value of practice in your life, you'll be motivated to make further discoveries—and then maintaining motivation will no longer be a problem. Motivation has to propel you into practice—but there it must stop. If you fill your sitting space with the desire for progress, you'll stifle your developing awareness. So letting go of motivation is critically valuable. When we sit, we should sit without purpose—without hope or fear.

Q: What about the motivation to liberate all sentient beings from the round of suffering?

NCR: That is a powerful motivating energy once we can tune in to it, but in order to generate kindness—to have genuinely attuned intent—we need to have some awareness of our interconnectedness. If we don't have (or if we're not conscious of having) kindness, we can't simply adopt it as an attitude because Lamas tell us it's a good idea. Kindness is our innate nature and needs to be discovered.

KD: We can imitate enlightenment by cultivating kindness in our thought and activity. . . . This will begin to open you to the discovery of beginningless kindness. But you'll need to sit and let go of constructs before you can really experience that. Genuine kindness is a truly effective motivation, but if you aren't able to feel it that strongly—if it doesn't permeate your view—how can it motivate you?

NCR: Remembering to generate kindness, or insinuating it into your mixed motivation, is a remarkable means of making sure that your kindness has a chance to develop. In this way it can become a more dominant factor within the pack of mongrel motivations that usually fill our silences with their barking.

Q: And when I sit—

NCR: When you sit—you *just sit*. You may generate kindness before you sit, but when you sit—you *just sit*. To consider the liberation of all beings as the driving force of motivation will not only keep your motivation aerodynamic, but will also ensure it's pointed in the right direction. Acquisitiveness mentality can also be aerodynamic in some respects, but we end up flying into high-intensity narrowness and frustration. Kindness can help us in our attitude toward sitting. But when we *are* sitting, there should be no motivation whatsoever. Motivation gets you to the cushion or stool, but then it has served its purpose. Your car takes you to the seaside, but if you want to go for a swim—you have to leave it behind.

Q: Could you say a little more about attuned intent? I'm finding this idea very helpful.

NCR: It's motivation without a "drag factor." It's streamlined—aerodynamic. It gives you access to incredible power and capacity for accomplishment of whatever needs to be accomplished. This is why generating kindness-thought and kindness-action is so vital. Kindness-intention cuts against the gravitational pull of divorced individuation. Divorced individuation is what keeps you earthbound. In order to accelerate into the unimaginable, we have to let go of the ballast—jettison the habits of view that create drag factors.

Q: I'm not exactly sure what you mean by drag factors; could you say a little more about that?

NCR: When our motivation is mixed, it can be said to have drag factors. I'll give an example. Say I want to help someone who is in need of help, but I also want to be seen as a good person. Wanting to be seen as a good person is a drag factor. If I want to be appreciated, thanked, and praised, then I'll be of less help than I could have been. I will have complicated a relatively simple situation. Because I've complicated it, it won't necessarily run smoothly. I may well be distracted from my helping by my desire for recognition. My motivation to help and my motivation for recognition could come into conflict. When motivations conflict there's a considerable drag factor, and when there's a drag factor . . . goals become much harder to reach. But this can also work the other way around. This is why I speak about insinuating kindness-intention into our unskillful motivation in order to undermine the process of distraction.

KD: In terms of reaching a goal, you could look at it this way: say I want to save money in order to go to the Himalayas. But I may also want to acquire new clothes. That would definitely eat into my savings. If I keep doing that, it would be a long time, if ever, before I got to be among the mountains.

NCR: This is what we'd call the drag factor—it's the thing that slows you down. Mixed and conflicting motivations produce a drag factor and inhibit our development and growth as human beings. As long as there's a drag factor, we experience frustration and the unsatisfactory outcome of our wishes or intentions, whatever they might be. Attuned intent is unmixed motivation, motivation without conflict—single-pointed motivation.

Kindness

Q: I want to ask about the need for developing compassion as the basis for realizing voidness. Your instruction on shi-nè turns that the other way around, which is different from the teachings I've heard before. That's been confusing me.

NCR: In one sense, this is part of the problem of dualism in general. What we have here is the contentious issue that realization can be discovered by methods that contradict each other—methods that are the reverse or mirror image of each other. If we don't understand that these methods are reflections of each other, we polarize them and interpret their respective angles as antagonistic to each other. This kind of paradox is common in Buddhism, and it points to something absolutely crucial. If enlightenment made sense from a relative standpoint, it would be a relative state of being. The fact that it's not possible to speak in relative terms about ultimate experience without using paradoxes is what defines the relative view as dualistic and the ultimate view as beyond dualism. The practice of generating compassion as the basis for realizing emptiness doesn't contradict the practice of realizing emptiness in order to discover the spontaneous compassion that springs from that realization. If we generate kindness, we imitate enlightenment, and in imitating enlightenment we facilitate the realization of emptiness. If we let go and let be through the practice of the Four Naljors, we discover that kindness is the spontaneous expression that is liberated by that unfolding.

KD: There is no reason at all why anyone shouldn't follow both practices—indeed we would advocate it. The main point is that you should understand the principles of these methods—you should understand how they function. Once you comprehend their individual characteristics—once you understand the ways in which these methods work—you stand the chance of being able to engage in them and realize something. If not, you'll just get into all kinds of tangles.

NCR: The wisdom of emptiness and the infinite compassionate activity that arises from it are not actually divisible, but from our dualistic perspective we divide them. Having divided wisdom and active compassion in this way, we devise means of realizing *either* through the practice of manifesting the *other*. This means that we either manifest wisdom through nonattachment to referentiality or we manifest kindness through contemplative thinking and processes of active imagination. The realization of both practices is that wisdom and active compassion are indivisible. Do you understand?

Q: Yes, thank you—I feel like I suddenly understood a lot! Everything suddenly fits into place! [*laughs*]

Q: Is compassion the same thing as love?

KD: They're aspects of the same energy.

NCR: Love and compassion as words or terms are framed by specific meanings that make them different in a relative sense. But love and compassion as aspects of the energy of enlightenment are divisionless. Love in the conventional sense of the word is different from the conventional sense of the word *compassion*, but from the viewpoint of realized reasoning they're undivided. Both love and compassion mean the experience of divisionlessness.

KD: It's not possible to experience either love or compassion if our sense of ourselves exists separately from our experience of others. When *your* pain and pleasure are to some extent *my* pain and pleasure, then you can call that love. If we extend that outward to encompass all living beings, then we call that compassion or kindness. Kindness is divisionless, and divisionlessness is enlightenment. Both love and compassion are free from the inhibitions and constrictions of self-orientation. Selfishness springs from a sense of dividedness, of being separate from the rest of the universe. Selfishness is our distorted sense of hyperindividuation, in which we imagine we can act on behalf of ourselves alone. We don't often seem to connect with the idea that if we love selectively or conditionally, it can all turn rather sour. For real love to exist, kindness needs to pervade our perception, which automatically means that we also know how to be kind to ourselves.

NCR: If we discover kindness within ourselves, then love can flower in radiant profusion. But if we contrive to generate a narrow, clinging possessiveness toward one person (to the exclusion of others), we cripple our capacity to manifest kindness.

Q: If you feel compassion for someone who has malicious intentions, don't you just leave yourself open to attack? How can you feel compassion for an enemy without becoming a victim?

NCR: Kindness isn't a simplistic pie-in-the-sky idiot grin. If people don't have your best interests at heart, you need to remain aware of their intentions. This doesn't mean that you can't wish them well— just that you don't wish them well at your expense.

KD: Until you lose the victim concept, you have to work within the scope of your limitations. Generating kindness toward people who may wish to victimize you is actually the very best means of protecting yourself. To feel compassion for people who want to hurt you, you need to try to understand *why* they want to hurt you. You also need to work out why it could be that they've come to feel ill-disposed toward you. One thing you can be fairly sure about is that they're only doing whatever it is that they're doing because they're trying to be happy. The fact that what makes them happy makes you sad is often overlooked because they've divided themselves from you and are unable to *feel* for *you*. If anyone seems to be out to put you down, you can be sure that they've got some pretty efficient rationalizations on the go. What's more, you can be fairly confident that they feel quite justified in their motivations and whatever schemes their rationale suggests. If you sincerely try to understand the pattern of their motivation, it becomes easier to feel compassion.

NCR: Kindness doesn't necessarily mean saying, "Hey, look! I'm going to lie on the ground so that you can stomp all over me! Hey! Why not try these golf shoes! They'd really make a mess of me."

KD: Kindness doesn't really constitute allowing or encouraging people to abuse you. If you encourage abuse, it only entrenches people in the belief that their behavior is somehow in order. It's not really compassionate to facilitate the development of distorted views in others, even if it gives us the dubious buzz of feeling like martyrs. Compassion includes *us*—we need to love and look after ourselves. If we have no love for ourselves, it's not possible to have compassion for others.

NCR: If our love for ourselves is so exclusive that we are only free to hate whoever is after our guts, then they're never likely to have a change of heart. But if we try to understand, if we keep an open heart, we might change the whole situation. We might be in a position to do some "enemy" a kindness, and if that can flow easily from us, we could transform enmity into harmony. But we need to be open-hearted—our kindness has to be nonexclusive, otherwise we're not likely to feel we have the capacity to be charitable.

Q: Is it that seeing everyone as striving for happiness in their own weird way is the key to being able to empathize with absolutely everything and everybody in the most compassionate way possible?

KD: Yes. That's very necessary. It's also necessary if you're to have compassion for yourself.

Q: Taking precautions and feeling compassion aren't incompatible then?

KD: Wisdom and compassion aren't incompatible either. You've got your common sense, you've even got your uncommon sense—your innate wisdom. We've got our everyday intelligence, and we need to allow that to function in the same way that our metabolism or blood circulation functions.

NCR: There's no particular value in a contrived naïveté that imagines everyone is mainly good, purely because it chooses to ignore their manifest negative complexes. Trying to understand where people are coming from naturally informs your dealings with them. If you haven't really got a clue why someone wants to stick one on you, you're unlikely to be able to sidestep an attack.

KD: If you've gained enough experience of practice to have developed your clarity, other people's motivation also becomes increasingly transparent. When people's motivation becomes transparent, they cease to be able to surprise you. If people are transparent to you, compassion is a natural reflex.

Q: What would you say to the idea that compassion is wasted on some people, because they would only mistake it as weakness?

KD: To mistake compassion for weakness is to be in a very pitiable state of mind. How could you *not* feel compassion for people who are so far removed from access to natural human warmth? That compassion can be considered to be weakness is no reflection on compassion. So, compassion that is concerned about being seen as weakness is maybe not really compassion at all. It's only possible to take advantage of weakness, but not of compassion. With compassion—with *great kindness*—there's no concept of being taken for a ride, because you're joy-riding anyway! Kindness, rather than being in any way weak, is actually enormously powerful because it flows from the indestructible nature of our being.

Q: Can you feel compassion for someone who pretends to be warm and friendly as a front for a self-seeking, cold, and ruthless interior—who pursues what he wants at the expense of everyone around him? Someone who cheats on his wife all the time and who's physically vicious with his wife? A man who lies, manipulates, and exploits others without regret?

NCR: I'd call that very isolated, frightened, and insecure—someone to be pitied. It's a matter of understanding that person's motivation.

KD: Why do you think such a person would want to be manipulative, exploitative, and violent?

Q: I don't know—that's just it, I don't know.

KD: Have you never been angry or arrogant, or done anything spiteful?

Q: Well, as a child and, well, yes—but I don't like myself when I feel like that.

KD: So you do understand a little. I mean, it's not as if there are people like Hitler and Stalin . . . and people like us, without a connection between the two.

NCR: If any of us were in the right place at the right time, and in the right frame of mind for becoming some sort of Hitler, Stalin, or Caligula clone, we'd understand even more about what the choices were. But it would be difficult to have an overview at that point—we couldn't stand outside what was happening and see what we were becoming through our choices.

KD: But think about what you just said: "I don't like myself when I feel like that." Part of your answer lies in that. You don't like yourself when you feel evil because you don't understand that feeling from the perspective of being who you usually are. So if we act spitefully, it's important to attempt to understand that manifestation of ourselves. If we just hate ourselves for how we behave, that acts as a wall between us and our understanding of what we are. The dislike for ourselves that we generate is really only a way of hiding from ourselves and obscuring the root fear, isolation, and insecurity that arises out of misconceiving the spaciousness of our being. We're usually afraid of what we don't understand, so it's rather important for us to face the distortions of our being in the practice of shi-nè.

NCR: We have to have sympathy for the devil—and sympathy for ourselves. If we have no sympathy for ourselves—if we fear our own negative feelings and wish to disown them—how can we have compassion for others? If our own "evil" feelings frighten us, we need to stare into them and gain knowledge of the nature of their arising. We cannot possibly understand an "evil" person if we remain a mystery to ourselves. If we have no knowledge of ourselves, then how can we include Hitler in our vow to liberate all beings?

KD: This is why sitting is so important. We have to confront what we are and acknowledge it before kindness can arise and flood the world with our unrestrained warmth.

Everyday Life

Q: I know this question asks for a long answer, but is there anything brief you could say about how to bring practice into my everyday life?

KD: By letting go of the sharp divisions between the times when you're sitting and the times when you're not sitting. Sitting is a little bit like going into retreat—it's a period of time when you completely let go of all involvement.

NCR: Sitting is a space in our lives where we can nurture our awareness, but awareness should manifest continuously.

KD: His Holiness Dudjom Rinpoche once said, "The initial experience of rigpa is rather like a baby thrown ruthlessly into the battlefield of arising phenomena." This means that you have to nurture the experience of awareness. It has to be integrated gently with every day. You can't just plunge back into your conventional existence if you're aiming at integration.

NCR: To integrate practice into everyday life, you should allow the spaciousness you discover in your sitting to overflow into your ordinary life experience. To make a metaphor: you must dismantle the dam that holds back the great ocean of being from flooding your existence. You can start by allowing the postpractice period to be a time when you remain completely *with* whatever you're doing.

Q: Is there a method—

NCR: No.

KD: There is no *method*. There's just being.

NCR: If there's a *method* then . . . ?

Q: Quite [*laughs*].

KD: If you want to develop the postmeditation experience, the *jé-thob* experience, you'll need to make sure that you leave time for it. If you sit for an hour, make sure that you have at least fifteen to thirty minutes for the jé-thob period. When you get up from your sitting session, stand up slowly and with awareness. Massage any pain or stiffness in your legs and ankles, and continue to find the presence of your awareness in whatever sensation arises—but avoid conceptualizing about the process.

NCR: Find the presence of your awareness in every nuance of your movements, but don't fall prey to internalization. Just be where you are.

KD: You could get up and make a cup of coffee. You could do the washing up. But whatever you do, simply be with what you're doing.

NCR: If you get distracted, simply return to presence of awareness.

KD: It's best to be on your own in the jé-thob period, so that you can integrate presence of awareness with each moment without too much external distraction. When your jé-thob time is up, don't let that end suddenly either. In the same way that you moved carefully from sitting into movement, move gradually from the jé-thob period into whatever it is that has to happen next. In fact, there's really no need to end the jé-thob session at all. We all continually lose presence, but whenever your presence reemerges and you realize that you've drifted off, you can remain in or with that presence.

NCR: This is the practice of everyday life—continually returning to presence whenever you are distracted from presence, and continuing with awareness to remain in that presence. The real practice of integration is to return to presence of awareness whenever you are distracted.

KD: This is in fact the practice of Dzogchen—the most direct practice of enlightenment, so maybe you can't practice like this. But maybe you can. But whatever your level of practice, you can try to be mindful of whatever it is you're doing.

Q: That seems almost too simple.

KD: Yes . . . almost.

Q: I feel as if there's nothing for me to get hold of in that, as if there should be something more.

NCR: Like something that would enable you to "be" in a particular style, rather than simply being?

Q: Oh . . . I see what you mean!

NCR: The method is a method of *no-method*. The method is *simply being*. If you find that you can't continue in that state of simply being, then you can try to be mindful.

Q: And if you can't be mindful?

KD: Then you trip over things. It's life's way of reminding us to be mindful.

NCR: From a Tantric perspective you could say that the *pawo*s and *khandro*s observe your lack of mindfulness and give you an ankle tap that sends you sprawling onto the ground [*laughs*].

KD: But if you can't be mindful, then maybe you can try to acknowledge what's going on around you *as* a teaching.

Q: Could you say a little more about seeing life as a teaching?

NCR: Well—you can let the world speak to you. You can listen to the world. You can see what the phenomenal world is mirroring.

KD: You can see impermanence, sickness, old age, and death all around you.

NCR: It's a free teaching.

KD: It's happening all the time, and all you have to do is observe it and take it in. You can understand from just looking at what's going on all around you that this is what life is. Sometimes it's happy, sometimes it's sad, and sometimes it can't quite seem to make up its mind.

NCR: But what is it that sees? What is the nature of your perception? Sometimes it's attracted, sometimes it's averse, and sometimes it's indifferent. And what *is* that focus to which you're either attracted, averse or indifferent? Who is it that finds himself or herself to be attracted, averse, or indifferent? It's simply spaciousness—the nature of what is.

KD: Maybe from this perspective you could discover the greater appropriateness of mirroring this suchness without judgment.

NCR: In order to acknowledge what is, you need to learn how to *see what is*. As soon as you deal with areas beyond conventional comprehension, words become stretched to capacity, and you either follow them or you don't. But you can always learn from life. You can walk down the street and let it be a contemplation on the nature of existence. You can allow your intrinsic warmth to arise in response to the sadness you see. You can allow yourself to feel open and loving toward the people you see passing you.

KD: Walking down the street can be a powerful experience if you actually take in what's going on.

Q: There's so little time for us here in the West, with job and family and so many demands. How is it possible to find peace and tranquillity in our lives?

KD: Do you think that the East and the West are so different?

Q: I'd think in a place like India there'd be a lot less pressure than here.

KD: They also have jobs and families. But what about those pressures? What kind of pressures are you talking about? You don't have to answer too personally if you'd rather not.

Q: No, it's not so personal. It's the pressure of society to achieve and to perform, and for your children to achieve and be successful.

KD: Sounds like India to me. But don't you have a choice as to whether you accept this pressure?

Q: It's expected.

KD: Well, yes, maybe—but what's the penalty if you don't do what's expected?

Q: You mean we should all just drop out?

KD: Why does that have to be the alternative?

NCR: That's simply a polarization.

Q: Well, what else is there?

KD: We don't see the situation as having to be polarized. I think you can drop out if you like. I think you can be a corporate executive if you like.

NCR: There's no problem with what you do. There's simply an issue around how you feel about it. There's no need to be a typical dropout or a typical executive, but I think that the penalty for being atypical can sometimes be isolation. If you interest yourself in anything outside the norm, you'll be going against the general trend. If you've been interested enough to come here tonight, and interested enough to come along on many other occasions, then you must have some freedom and independence from the norm already. All the people here are really free enough to be individuals and write their own scripts for how they'll live their lives. Some of the choices you make are bound to set you apart from one social group or another.

KD: It's not really possible to live creatively if you're governed by what's expected of you. What happens when people close to you expect opposite things from you? What do you do then? It's really not possible to please all the people all the time. Choices have to be made, directions have to be taken, and you have to accept the whole situation in terms of the person you're becoming.

Q: But I feel that if I lived in a place where spiritual values were important and honored, there'd be less conflict. At least the slower pace of life in India must make it easier to meditate.

NCR: That depends on who you are. It depends on the style of how you experience your life. What really matters is that enlightenment is our beginningless nature—we're all practicing in order to realize that. I'm practicing to realize that. We all have flashes of our beginningless enlightenment from time to time. You too.

KD: For some of us that experience is more frequent—for others less frequent, but we all practice to increase the frequency and intensity of the sparkling through which is our innate enlightenment. It's not the environment that makes the difference, it's the state of mind.

NCR: I can see that there seems to be a sense of spiritual romance about the East.

KD: That's a fantasy balloon that needs to be punctured.

NCR: Absolutely. The idea that India is a peaceful place is a little misleading. Sure . . . there are peaceful tracts of the Himalayas. There are places there that have a wonderful atmosphere for practice. But then, if you go to the highlands of Scotland or somewhere like that, you'll find equally wonderful places. In India, wherever there are people, there's usually also quite a lot of noise and bustle. I remember sitting in a quiet place in the woods above McLeod Ganj. A more tranquil spot you couldn't hope to find—but it wasn't long before a conspicuous party of Indian tourists arrived to have a picnic about two hundred yards away from me. Now our idea of a picnic may be to go off to some remote and idyllic spot to immerse ourselves in the beauty or grandeur of the scenery. But the popular Indian alternative is a bit different. It gives them more pleasure to turn a woodland glen into an open-air nightclub. I'm making no serious value judgment here, but I know which kind of picnic I'd find more appealing. I think that the industrial environment in which many of us live gives us more of a taste for the beauty of nature than our rather more festive Indian friends. They often love nothing better than to have half a dozen radios wound up to capacity emitting the most fiendish row. Have you ever heard Hindi film music? [*laughs*] One thing that being in India certainly did for me was to push my nose hard up against the reality of death. And it wasn't just the sight of a Ganges hippo that did that, it was the sheer closeness to death of everything.

KD: It was the way that in that heat and humidity buildings would be showing signs of decay before they were even finished.

Q: Pardon me, Rinpoche, did you say hippos? In the Ganges?

NCR: Sorry, I should explain about the Ganges hippo. When human bodies have been immersed in water for long enough, they swell up and become almost unrecognizable as human beings. In my day, people called them Ganges hippos. India is hardly a peaceful place. The best place for practice *has* to be wherever you live, otherwise the path we're discussing would merely be a cultural manifestation. The practice of sitting is transcultural—it deals with the human condition in all its diversity. The tall pointed hats with long earflaps worn by Lamas represent the retreat cave. The meaning of this is that your retreat is *wherever you are*. In the noisiest place imaginable—there is silence. Sound manifests within *silent* space, and the function of practice is to discover silent mind. When mind is silent, there is endless silent space in which sounds sing infinitely separate songs.

KD: Even if you were to find yourself a retreat cave high in the Himalayas, or sit in a soundproof room, you'd start to hear the sounds of your own body. There'd be fluids gurgling. There'd be the sound of your breathing and the background hiss of your ears. These sounds would eventually distract and disturb you as much as any other sounds. You'd be disturbed by this simply because you'd never come to terms with the dissonance of your own subconscious noise. Body sounds would seem as offensive as the din of London traffic. People often say that they'd like to meditate but there never seems to be enough peace and quiet. They say, "If only I could go and live in the country, I'd be able to settle into a meditative lifestyle." I'm sorry to say that this is just another fanciful idea. The countryside is as full of distracting noises as anywhere else. The sound of a pneumatic drill in the street below your bedroom window or the sound of several thousand crickets—which would be more distracting? Sure, the crickets aren't there all year round, but then neither is the pneumatic drill.

NCR: I gave a course once at a Buddhist center, and the most profound meditative experience anyone had was when a road resurfacing machine passed by below. I heard it coming, and just as it started to annoy the people sitting, I said, "Just find the presence of your awareness in the dimension of the sound." And they did. It was a wonderful sound. The sound of rooks roosting can be very intrusive—much more so than the hum of distant traffic. The "natural world" has romantic associations for you, but ultimately it comes down to concept—it's a matter of your attraction, aversion, and indifference to what these various sounds represent rather than to the energy of the sound itself. To imagine that a peaceful place makes meditation easier is ultimately nonsensical.

Q: So you'd be better off accepting whatever situation you find yourself in.

NCR: Exactly. Wherever you are is exactly where *you are*, and where can you be apart from where you are?

KD: If you have to alter your location to realize you're not unenlightened, it means that the method you've chosen is limited by circumstantial conditions. But if you take the relative view, there are a few things I could say that might apply to how you happen to find yourself in relation to daily practice. If you have extensive experience in practice, you can sit anywhere and integrate the presence of your awareness with whatever arises as a sense perception. But when you're new to practice, you need to treat yourself a little more gently and take account of the fact that you can easily become distracted. Now this may sound as if I'm contradicting what I said before, and to some extent I am—because ultimate view and relative view often appear to conflict.

NCR: Our initial comments dealt with the fact that there's no such thing as a distracting influence. This is the ultimate view. You distract yourself—you can't blame the noises, as they have no volition or distracting intention in themselves. I made this point in order to discredit the idea that you have to find some peaceful, tranquil spot before you can sit. But from a relative point of view, you do have to find a situation where you're not intruded upon by noises that have a regular or intelligible pattern. What I mean by this is that if there's someone next door and they have cranked up their radio on some manic, fast-talking commercial music show, it can be very difficult to keep yourself from tuning in to it. If the couple next door are having a shrill acrimonious row and your walls aren't particularly thick, trying to let go and let be can be tricky.

Q: According to recent statistics, the number-one cause of Britons' complaining about noise nuisance from the neighbors relates to excessive screaming during intercourse.

KD: Really? How delightful . . . that should be a cause of applause rather than complaint.

NCR: I guess that would also give you something to stick to in terms of concept . . .

KD: Or even conception [*laughs*]. Still, I'm always glad to hear about happiness. Anyhow . . . the problems lie in the intelligible quality of the sound rather than its volume. Traffic hum and the chirping of crickets are unintelligible sounds, and you should be able to get along with that kind of sound in most of its manifestations. With unintelligible sounds there's not so much for your intellect to latch on to. Because these sounds aren't deliberately fabricated by intellect (and because they have no discernible intellectual content), intellect doesn't key in to them unless you overlay them with concepts of like or dislike.

NCR: The intellectual faculties lock like Velcro onto intellectually produced sound unless you have considerable meditative stability. So if you have to battle to keep your attention off intellectual noise, it can become a bit like trying to swim with a few fur coats on.

Q: Can it be dangerous to meditate in everyday situations—for example, driving a car?

KD: It largely depends on what you mean by meditation. If you find the presence of your awareness in dimension of the process of driving, you'll be the safest driver on the road.

NCR: If your mind is wandering, if your attention is not on what you're doing, if you're hang gliding in your imagination while you drive, that could certainly be very dangerous. Have you ever seen those stickers in the back of cars that say things like "I'd rather be windsurfing"? I think that the Buddhist version could run "I'd rather be precisely where I am."

KD: Often people are off somewhere else, even when they're windsurfing. If your meditation is something like a trance state in which you enter some other world and cut off the outside world, then yes, that could be lethal. But that's not the kind of meditation we've been talking about. We've been explaining the practice of maintaining your presence of awareness—being completely *with* whatever you're doing.

NCR: In this way, driving your car *is* the practice. The idea that the Four Naljors cut you off from the "outside world" dies hard, so I must emphasize that whatever methods of meditation are taught in other systems, these Naljors are *not* about turning inward. There's no inward or outward bias in these practices—just being, in order to heal the dividedness of inner and outer.

The Confederate Sanghas of Aro

THE CONFEDERATE SANGHAS of Aro are linked groups of *gö-kar-'i dé chang-lo* or *ngak'phang* practitioners in the United Kingdom, United States, and Europe under the guidance of Ngak'chang Rinpoche and Khandro Déchen, the lineage-holders of the Aro gTér; they are under the spiritual direction of Nga-la Rig'dzin Dorje, Ngakma Nor'dzin Pamo, and Ngakpa 'ö-Dzin Tridral. The ngak'phang, or white tradition lineages, of the Nyingma School are sometimes known as the householder or nonmonastic traditions. The color white has an array of meanings that apply to those whose practice is based primarily in the Tantras. In Tibet, white is commonly regarded as a color worn by laypeople, and therefore connotes that the wearers are not monks or nuns (who wear red or maroon), although they are ordained practitioners. White is also the color of purity—the color of undyed cloth. As a Tantric symbol, white relates to the aspect of practice in which nothing has to be renounced at the outer level, because everything is regarded as intrinsically pure—pure from beginninglessness. The lineages of the ngak'phang tradition owe their inspiration to Padmasambhava and Yeshé Tsogyel (the Tantric Buddhas) and teach, more than any other tradition, integration of practice with everyday life. Many great siddhas and accomplished masters in these lineages have been nomads, farmers, or craftspeople. Some have lived as hidden yogis and yoginis, with nobody knowing who they were. There have been great teachers who have been illiterate yet

whose teachings have occupied scholars for centuries. Many important Lamas of this tradition, both men and women, have been family
people whose lives have demonstrated the essence of the teaching in
its most profound respects. The teachings and practice style of the
white tradition can obviously be of immense benefit to people in the
West today. The Confederate Sanghas of Aro have been established
to make this tradition more accessible.

Sang-ngak-chö-dzong, the first of the Aro sanghas, was established
in 1977. It was given its name by H.H. Jigdral Yeshé Dorje Dudjom
Rinpoche as an inspiration for the establishment of a ngak'phang
sangha in the West. Since then other Aro sanghas have been estab-
lished as charitable organizations in the United States (Aro Gar),
Austria (Aro Gesellschaft), and Germany (Aro Gemeinschaft).
Ngak'chang Rinpoche and Khandro Déchen teach regularly in
Britain and the United States (New York and California) where they
have personal students. A few of their senior disciples also teach and
have their own apprentices: Nga-la Rig'dzin Dorje in Europe and
Scandinavia, and Ngakma Nor'dzin Pamo and Ngakpa 'ö-Dzin
Tridral in Britain.

Ngak'chang Rinpoche and Khandro Déchen wish to establish the
Confederate Sanghas of Aro as a happy, creative environment in
which the qualities of human warmth and friendliness are paramount
and extended to all who wish to practice and participate in the enact-
ment of vision. They hope to encourage the creative talents of the
individual, to pass on skills, and to provide a rich variety of supports
for practice.

For further information on the ngak'phang tradition, open teachings and retreats, or apprenticeship with the Aro Lamas, please visit
our website at http://www.aroter.org or write to:

Sang-ngak-chö-dzong
P.O. Box 65, Penarth
Vale of Glamorgan CF64 1XY
U. K.

Aro Gar
P.O. Box 330
Ramsey, NJ 07446
U.S.A.

Aro Gesellschaft
Am Forst 17
A-7212 Forchtenstein
Austria

Aro Gemeinschaft
An den Hueren 99
D-41066 Moenchengladbach
Germany

Glossary

Note: This glossary shows two different transliteration systems for Tibetan words. The most commonly used spelling comes first, with the less common spelling in parentheses. In addition, unless noted otherwise, all non-English words are in Tibetan.

Aro gTér (a ro gTer)   The visionary treasures of Aro. The revealed teachings of the female gTértön Kyungchen Aro Lingma, received in vision from Yeshé Tsogyel.

Aro Lingma (a ro gLing ma)   1886–1923. Female Nyingma gTértön (discoverer of visionary revelation teachings), who received the Aro gTér in vision directly from Yeshé Tsogyel.

Aro Naljor-zhi (a ro rNal 'byor bZhi)   The Four Naljors of the Aro gTér. The *ngöndro* (preliminary practices) of Dzogchen Sem-dé. Four practices of silent sitting meditation: shi-nè, lha-tong, nyi'mèd, lhun-drüp.

bodhicitta (Skt.; Tib. byang chub sems)   Literally, "buddha mind." Active compassion.

Dzogchen (rDzogs chen)   The innermost of the three inner Tantras, based on the principle of self-liberation. Literally, "Great Completion." This indicates that the enlightened state does not have to be added to in any way—it is complete in itself from beginninglessness.

Four Naljors (Tib. rNal 'byor bZhi)   The *ngöndro* (preliminary practices) of Dzogchen Sem-dé: shi-nè, lha-tong, nyi'mèd, lhun-drüp.

gö-kar chang-lo'i dé (gos dKar lCang lo'i sDe)   Literally, "white skirt, long (or braided) hair series," it refers to the manner of dress of ordained ngak'phang practitioners.

gomchen/gomchenma (sGom chen/sGom chen ma)   Meditation master.

gYo-wa (gYo ba)   Movement, "that which moves." The experience in which one becomes completely identified with the movement of whatever arises in mind.

lha-tong (lhag mThong)   The method of reintegrating the presence of awareness with the movement of whatever arises in Mind.

lhun-drüp (lhun grub)   Spontaneous self-perfectedness, experience of nondual presence of awareness in every moment.

Long-dé (kLong sDe)   The Series of Space, one of the three series of Dzogchen.

Marpa (mar pa) 1012–1097.   Marpa Lotsawa (the translator) was the Lama of Milarépa.

Me-ngag-dé (man ngag sDe)   The Series of Implicit Instruction, one of the three series of Dzogchen.

Milarépa (mi la ras pa) 1052–1135.   A great yogi famous for his songs of realization and for his accomplishment of the practice of *tu-mo* (psychic heat yoga).

mi-thog-pa (mi rTog pa)   The state of no content of mind, no mental manifestations, no *namthogs*.

naljor (rNal 'byor)   Remaining in the natural state.

nalma (rNal ma)   Exhaustion, in the sense of exhaustion of neurotic involvement with thought as a definition of being; relaxation into the natural state.

namthog (rNam rTog)   That which arises in Mind. A *namthog* could be anything, not simply thoughts but patterns, colours, textures, and feelings.

nè-pa (gNas pa)   Absence with presence. The state in which there is absence of thought but presence of awareness.

ngakpa/ngakma (sNgags pa/sNgags ma)   Literally, "mantra man" or "mantra woman." A practitioner of Vajrayana who has taken Tantric vows.

ngak'phang (sNgags 'phang)   Literally, "mantra-wielding." A non-monastic, noncelibate tradition of ordained yogis and yoginis who integrate practice with everyday life.

ngöndro (sNgon 'gro)   Literally, "before going." Preliminary practices.

nyi'mèd (gNyis med)   Literally, "nondual." Indivisibility, the recognition of the one taste of emptiness and form.

Nyingma (rNying ma)   The "Ancient" school, one of the four schools of Tibetan Buddhism, brought to Tibet by Padmasambhava in the eighth century. A heterodox stream of many different lineages characterized by diversity of style and approach.

Padmasambhava (Skt.; Tib. pad ma 'byung gNas)   The male Tantric Buddha and spiritual consort of Yeshé Tsogyel who introduced the Buddhist teachings to Tibet in the eighth century.

rigpa (rig pa)   Instant presence, nondual awareness, presence of awareness, nondual presence.

ro-chig (ro gCig)   Literally, "one taste." The experience of emptiness and form as nondual—having the same taste (experiential quality).

sem (sems)   Ordinary conceptual mind.

Sem-dé (sems sDe)   The Series of the nature of Mind, one of the three series of Dzogchen.

sem-nyid (sems nyid)   The nature of Mind, the empty quality of Mind, the space in which *sem* arises and enters into either compassionate communication or dualistic contrivances.

shi-nè (zhi gNas)   The method of finding oneself in the space of Mind without content while maintaining presence of awareness.

Sutra (Skt.; Tib. mDo)   Discourses and teachings by Shakyamuni Buddha having their basis in the principle of renunciation.

Tantra (Skt.; Tib. rGyud) Literally, "continuity" or "thread." The teachings of Buddhism which have as their basis the principle of transformation.

vajra (Skt.; Tib. rDo rJe) Literally "lord stone." Indestructible, thunderbolt, diamond.

Vajrayana (Skt.; Tib. rDo rJe theg pa) The Indestructible Vehicle, the Diamond Vehicle. The Buddhist practices of the inner Tantras.

Yeshé Tsogyel (ye shes mTsho rGyal) The female Tantric Buddha, spiritual consort of Padmasambhava and the origin of the Aro gTér.

yogi/yogini (Skt.; Tib. rNal 'byor pa/rNal 'byor ma) Male and female Vajrayana practitioners of the spatial yogas; one who rests in the natural state.

Index

Printed in the United States
by Baker & Taylor Publisher Services